Sea la Luz

EL METODISTA.

Mensual en el interes de la Religion, Moralidad, Educacion, y Temperancia.

Thomas Harwood,
EDITOR.

J. A. Lowe
DIRECTOR

AÑO 3. SOCORRO, NUEVO MEXICO, FREBERO. DE 1888. NO. 4.

"Sea la Luz"

"Sea la luz" was a motto on the banner of both the *Metodista Neo-Mexicano* and *El Metodista* published in New Mexico during the 1880s by Thomas Harwood. It is a quote from Genesis 1:3 ("Let there be light") and is a reflection of the Protestant understanding of the role of their message.

Sea la Luz

THE MAKING OF MEXICAN PROTESTANTISM IN THE AMERICAN SOUTHWEST, 1829–1900

Juan Francisco Martínez

Number 4 in the Al Filo:
Mexican American Studies Series

University of North Texas Press
Denton, Texas

10 9 8 7 6 5 4 3 2 1

Permissions:
University of North Texas Press
P.O. Box 311336
Denton, TX 76203-1336

The paper used in this book meets the minimum requirements of the American National Standard for Permanence of Paper for Printed Library Materials, z39.48.1984. Binding materials have been chosen for durability.

Library of Congress Cataloging-in-Publication Data

Martinez, Juan Francisco, 1957–
    Sea la luz : the making of Mexican Protestantism in the American Southwest, 1829–1900 / Juan Francisco Martinez.
        p. cm. — (Al filo: Mexican American studies series ; no. 4)
    Includes bibliographical references and index.
    ISBN-13: 978-1-57441-222-2 (cloth : alk. paper)
    ISBN-10: 1-57441-222-1 (cloth : alk. paper)
        1. Mexican American Protestants—Southwest, New—History—19th century. 2. Southwest, New—Church history—19th century. I. Title. II. Series: Al filo ; no. 4.
    BR563.M49M33 2006
    280'.40896872079—dc22
                                                                            2006011180

Sea la Luz: The Making of Mexican Protestantism in the American Southwest, 1829–1900 is Number 4 in the Al Filo: Mexican American Studies Series

En memoria de:

Ana Gregoria García
Anita García
Juanita Guerra

Tatarabuela, bisabuela y abuela,
mujeres que se convirtieron a la fe evangélica
en México y Texas y que influyeron
en mi propio compromiso de seguir
a Cristo Jesús y de servir a otros en su nombre.

Contents

Illustrations

Abbreviations

BAP   American Baptist Convention (Northern)

BGC   Baptist General Convention (Southern)

MEC   Methodist Episcopal Church

MECS   Methodist Episcopal Church, South

PCUS   Presbyterian Church in the United States (Southern)

PCUSA   Presbyterian Church in the United States of America (Northern)

Preface

THIS BOOK WAS BORN IN THE LATINO PROTESTANT COMMUNITY.
Los *aleluyas*, as Latino Protestants were once called, often
made their commitment to follow Jesus Christ at great social
cost. Because they are a small minority within an ethnic minority, the story of their origins has often been lost, or ignored, by
both American Protestants and Latinos. Published works about
Mexicans and Mexican Americans in the nineteenth-century
Southwest largely ignore Spanish-speaking Protestants, either
making no mention of them at all or seeing this population as
a very marginal part of the community. The little material that
exists is written primarily by Protestants and usually includes
only a small section on the nineteenth century as part of a larger
work. The few exceptions tend to focus on the Protestant missionaries and not on the converts. Thus, this book began as a
dissertation that addressed this gap in the history of Latinos
and the Latino Protestant churches of the southwestern United
States.[1] At the same time, the gap in the historical accounts is
also a gap in my own story. The Mexican American Protestants
of the American Southwest are my forebearers and have made
me who I am. This is an attempt to tell a part of their story.

The bulk of the statistical data and basic information about
church and mission locations and leaders in this book come
from the denominational statistical records of the data reported
by their missionaries and churches. Other sources include articles in denominational and home mission periodicals, missionaries' reports and memoirs (particularly those by Melinda

Rankin and Thomas Harwood[2]), conference and synodal minutes, home mission publications, and Spanish-language periodicals and tracts. Finally, biographies and biographical notes
were written during the first part of the twentieth century about
three nineteenth-century Mexican American Protestants: José
Ynés Perea, Gabino Rendón, and José Policarpo Rodríguez.[3]
This means that the primary sources for understanding nineteenth-century Mexican American Protestants are the Anglo
American Protestant missionaries. So, though the goal is to tell
the story of the Spanish-speaking converts, it is mostly medi-
ated through the perspective of the missionaries, and their interpretation of the missionary encounter between themselves and
the Mexicans of the nineteenth-century American Southwest.

Many scholars have addressed aspects of the encounter between Mexican Americans and Protestant missionaries in the
nineteenth-century Southwest. Randi Walker (*Protestantism in
the Sangre de Cristos 1850–1920*, University of New Mexico
Press, 1991) analyzed Protestant mission work among the Spanish speaking in the Sangre de Cristos Mountains of northern
New Mexico and southern Colorado. Susan Yohn (*A Contest of
Faiths*, Cornell University Press, 1995) studied the work of the
Presbyterian missionary teachers in the same region. Others,
such as Colin Goodykoontz, Ferenc Szasz, and Mark Banker,
have addressed aspects of this encounter within the larger framework of Protestant Home Missions in the Southwest.

Many people were crucial to this effort. Paul Pierson, my
dissertation mentor, encouraged me and also gave me the freedom to develop this project. Justo González helped me keep the
research within the larger framework of Latino Protestant his-
toriography. Randi Walker's research and counsel provided important pointers during my research. I am particularly indebted
to Minerva and Pablo Garza, longtime Methodist pastors and
leaders in Texas, whose extensive experience helped me understand Latino Methodist history. Also, I am grateful to Leslie

Hawthorne Kingler and Susan Carlson Wood for their careful reading and editing of the manuscript.

My parents, Juan and Bertha Martínez, modeled a commitment to pastoral service in the Latino community and to excellence in study, even though their own opportunities for formal education were limited. They taught me to be proud of my Latino and Protestant heritage and of Spanish, the language they taught and nurtured in me. *¡Muchas gracias!*

Most importantly, I am indebted to my wife, Olga, and my children, Xaris and Josué. They encouraged me not to give up when progress was slow, and they sacrificed family time so that I could research and write.

Introduction

THE CONQUEST THAT TOOK FROM MEXICO THE TERRITORY THAT IS today the southwestern United States made approximately 100,000 Spanish-speaking people into U.S. citizens. These new citizens were Roman Catholic and represented American Protestants' first significant opportunity to preach to Spanish-speaking Catholics on the American continent. The tensions and relationships that developed in that interaction continue to this day. As the Latino community continues to grow and as a growing number of Latinos become Protestant,[1] the issues raised during the nineteenth century become even more pertinent. Historians, sociologists, and church leaders will find that the nineteenth-century story seems strangely contemporary. The relationship between conversion to Protestantism and cultural assimilation, the role of religion in cultural identity maintenance and inter-ethnic relations between Latinos and larger American society are all issues that began when the Mexicans north of the Rio Grande became American citizens in 1848. How those issues were addressed in the past speaks volumes to how they are being addressed today.

Latino Protestants, as a distinct ethno-religious group, were born in the midst of this encounter. These converts found spiritual vitality in their new faith, even as they struggled to define their space within both the Latino Catholic and the Anglo American Protestant communities. Their experiences continue to play themselves out in the borderlands of the Southwest as millions of Latinos continue to live in the midst of the legacy of that conquest.[2]

Many Protestants opposed the Mexican-American War (1846–1848) that resulted in the conquest of the Southwest. Others justified it by stating that a U.S. victory would open new evangelistic opportunities in the conquered territories and Mexico. Once the Treaty of Guadalupe Hidalgo (1848) placed the Southwest in U.S. control, many Protestant leaders who originally opposed the war also began to see it as the opening of a new mission field. This raised the question of the relationship between the nationalist agenda of a powerful nation and the missional goals of a church that reaps the benefits of being a part of that nation, an issue very much alive in the United States today.

Protestant desires to evangelize these Mexican Catholics who were now U.S. citizens were only a small chapter of a much larger effort by Protestant missionaries. Anglo American Protestants were convinced of the superiority of Protestantism over Catholicism. They were also sure that God was blessing the United States because of its Protestant heritage. The western expansion was a clear sign, for them, that God had a special mission for the United States. Yet the conquest of the Southwest also occurred in the midst of the growing migration of Catholics from Europe. Many Protestants were afraid that Catholics would not be good American citizens and that they would subvert God's blessing. Particularly, they were afraid that the Catholics had a primary allegiance to a foreign potentate (the pope) and that they would never give full allegiance to the United States. Therefore, Protestants had the duty, both as Christians and as Americans, to evangelize Catholics in the United States. Mexican Catholics, they believed, were one more group of people who were now American citizens who did not have the truth of Protestant faith and who could threaten the future of the United States if they did not become Protestants.

Protestant missionaries interpreted Mexican Catholicism in the Southwest within this broader understanding. As one reads how the missionaries understood Mexican Catholicism, it is clear that they did not understand the distinctives of this faith expression, nor its role in the social structures of the region. Many of their descriptions are clearly wrong, and many more provide a very distorted picture of Mexican Catholicism. Yet they are a faithful reflection of their understanding of the theological and cultural superiority of Protestant Christianity.

Nonetheless, this new evangelistic opportunity brought on by the end of the war with Mexico did not usher in a major mission effort among the Mexicans who remained in the Southwest. The handful of missionaries who went into the Southwest prior to the Civil War either abandoned their work for various reasons or saw little lasting evidence of their endeavors. The Mexican community did not readily accept Protestantism, and there were very few converts during the early years. After the Civil War several denominations pursued mission work in the region, though their efforts were relatively small. Despite some significant results, the end of the nineteenth century showed little possibility that strong Protestant churches would soon develop in the community. By 1900 there were only 150 Spanish-language Protestant congregations with a reported total of 5,632 adult church members in the Southwest. Yet these converts represented the beginning of a Latino Protestant identity and would play an important role in Protestantism's later expansion among Latinos throughout the Southwest and beyond.

During the nineteenth century a complex set of issues influenced Protestant mission efforts among Mexican Americans. These endeavors were shaped by Protestants' view of their mission and role in America, adaptation mechanisms used by the Mexicans to survive as a conquered people, and the influence of the broader American (Protestant) society on the Mexican American population. Each of these elements affected both the motivation and message of the Protestant missionaries, as well as the response to their efforts. But these efforts also took place within the larger context of the conquest of the Southwest that both provided the opportunity for the Protestant missionaries and limited their impact.

This book examines the Protestant mission efforts among the Mexicans who remained in the territory conquered from Mexico from the time of the first missionary contacts in the late 1820s through the end of the nineteenth century. Though these people became American citizens as a result of the Treaty of Guadalupe Hidalgo (1848), they were treated as foreigners in their own land. In nineteenth-century Protestant literature they were usually referred to as Mexicans or Spanish speaking. Toward the end of the period a few documents began to refer to them as Mexican Americans. To avoid anachronistic references, the terms *Mexican, Mexican American,* and *Spanish speaking* are used throughout to refer to the nineteenth-century population in general, and *tejano, neomejicano,* and *californio* are used to refer to those from a specific region. The term *Latino* is only used when referring to the larger community in the United States today, consisting partly of the descendants of those conquered during the nineteenth century.

Chapters One and Two offer a historical and social perspective on Protestant mission work among Mexican Americans by reviewing Protestant attitudes toward the U.S. conquest of the Southwest from Mexico and toward Mexicans during the nineteenth century. Chapter Three analyzes Protestant motives for evangelizing Mexicans in the Southwest. Chapters Four through Seven look at the Protestant missionary efforts and their impact in the Mexican American communities of the Southwest. Chapter Eight provides a description of Mexican American Protestants in the nineteenth century based on the limited available original sources. The conclusion places the nineteenth century beginnings within the larger story of the growth of Latino Protestantism in the Southwest.

Early Mexican American Protestant converts were at the margins of both their broader ethnic and religious communities. Mexican American Catholics rejected them because they had become Protestants. They had little control over the structures and symbols of Protestant faith, yet they began developing an identity that was both Mexican American and Protestant. The new Borderlands of the Southwest created the space for a new religious understanding even as it placed many pressures on its development.

Latino Protestants in the United States no longer have to deal with persecution or overt isolation from the larger Latino community. But the tensions related to being Latino and Protestant in the United States continue. Issues like cultural assimilation, identity maintenance, immigration, and relations with Latino Catholics and with the larger American population continue to be crucial for Latino Protestants in the Borderlands. Being both Latino and Protestant continues to be a dynamic identity whose boundaries are not easily defined nor maintained.

1

"Planting the Institutions of Freedom"

PROTESTANT ATTITUDES TOWARD THE CONQUEST OF THE SOUTHWEST

———◆◆◇◆◆———

Our country, right or wrong!

1840s popular slogan

The conquered hate the conquerors, and all that belongs to them, and very reluctantly, if ever, will they adopt their religious beliefs, social usages, forms and government, arts and sciences, and methods of advancement, except by stern compulsion.
  Abiel Livermore, *The War with Mexico Revisited* (1850)

THE MEXICAN-AMERICAN WAR (1846–1848) GENERATED OPPOSITION and protest from many Anglo American Protestants.[1] A strong antiwar sentiment in many churches led to denunciations of the United States' aggression against Mexico. Opposition to the war, however, did not necessarily imply disagreement with its principal goal: territorial expansion. Many Protestant leaders strongly opposed the war, but most supported the conquest of the Southwest.

6

Protestant Views on the Mexican-American War

The war with Mexico occurred during a time of growing tension in the United States. Slavery was dividing the country; Westward migration was moving the center of power from East to West; settlement of the Oregon Territory and the annexation of Texas heightened the possibility of war with Great Britain. All of these events were occurring in the midst of a broader debate about the identity of the United States.[2] Each of these issues colored people's attitudes toward the Mexican-American War and, for many, seemed to overshadow it in importance. For many Protestants the relationship of the war to these other issues was as important as the actual hostilities.

Opposition to the Mexican-American War

The strongest Protestant statements opposing the war with Mexico appear in denominational periodicals and published sermons. These critical and often scathing denunciations reflect a wide range of concerns about the conflict. Nonetheless, few denominations issued official pronouncements against the war. Those that were made usually reflected a pacifist stance. The strongest antiwar declarations came from the Unitarians.[3] Several other groups also published declarations against the war. Baptists in New York stated that "the spirit of war is contrary to, and utterly forbidden by the teaching and spirit of the Gospel."[4] Congregationalists called the war an "unchristian and most pernicious custom."[5] Presbyterians did not condemn the war directly, but called for its quick end due to "the great and dreadful evils of war."[6]

Many individuals, however, made pronouncements against the war. The Unitarian and Quaker periodicals, *Christian Register* and *Friends' Weekly Intelligencer,* published most of them.[7] But antiwar statements were also made by others, including Charles Hodge, who called on the 1846 Presbyterian

General Assembly "to confess before him [God] those nation's sins, which have provoked this national judgment."[8]

Nevertheless, most Protestant opposition to the war was due to its impact on other issues. For Protestants from the North and Northeast the most important issue was slavery. Many saw the war as a Southern effort to obtain new territories that could eventually become slave states. They saw the issue not so much as the war itself, but as the expansion of slavery into the Southwest.[9] The precedent was already set: Texas had been annexed in order to strengthen slavery. Congregationalist pastor Samuel Harris declared in his 1847 Thanksgiving sermon that "the present war [with Mexico], as is well known, is a consequence of that annexation. Therefore it is a war which slavery has brought upon us."[10] Abiel Livermore of the American Peace Society continued to reflect this sentiment after the war ended: "[T]he paramount cause and motive of the war with Mexico, without doubt or controversy, was territorial aggrandizement, under the dominion of domestic slavery and the internal slave trade."[11]

Regional tensions were also involved. New England Protestants like John Morison were concerned by what they saw as a national thirst for territorial expansion.[12] Presbyterian leader Albert Barnes lamented that "the territory [to be conquered] . . . would make seventy-two States of the same dimensions [as Massachusetts]"[13] which would change the states' balance of power. Westward expansion and the new statehood of large territories were diluting the traditional power of New England.

Samuel Harris was also concerned about the effects of the war on the population and the government. He stated that it was creating a love of conquest and pushing the country toward despotism, as reflected in the maxim *Our country, right or wrong*, which had become popular at the time.[14] It was also creating changes in the United States that would negatively impact the country. "[B]y increasing the dissimilarity of our population and the diversity of our local interest, by leading to a larger standing army, and by the direct and indirect military influence of the conquest, [this] must make our government more difficult to be administered and our liberties more precarious."[15]

Thomas Thomas, another Congregationalist minister, warned that war hostilities were producing a situation where there would be "an end to all law but that which is promulgated at the cannon's mouth."[16] American soldiers were committing atrocities such that an anonymous contributor to the *Christian Register* suggested that it might be better to send convicts to fight with Mexico—their moral conduct would be no worse than that of the soldiers.[17]

Antiwar Protestants argued that, contrary to what many believed, the war with Mexico would not help the "backward" Mexicans or expand republican and Protestant principles. In his 1847 Thanksgiving sermon Congregationalist pastor Burdett Hart stated that instead of encouraging Mexico to model itself after the United States, the war of conquest was providing a bad example.[18] Livermore reminded Americans that "the conquered hate the conquerors, and all that belongs to them."[19]

Support for the War

In spite of the significant opposition, some Anglo Protestants supported the Mexican-American War. Protestant publications did not strongly present the pro-war arguments, however, probably because they were defended in the press and were the government's official position. Nonetheless, there were Protestants who spoke in favor of the war. Most were part of Southern denominations or groups with a large stake in the expansion into the Southwest.

The advocates gave several reasons for the war effort. One of the most persistent arguments was that of self-defense. According to this view, Mexico had started the war with the United

States by killing "American soldiers on American soil."[20] There-fore, the country had the right to defend itself and should have been wary of peace societies that questioned this responsibility. Thomas Smyth, a Southern Presbyterian pastor, denounced "a wild enthusiastic philanthropy which attempts to be wiser and more merciful than God; to mend His ways; and to extirpate by methods of man's devising, evils which arise from the necessary derangement into which sin has plunged the world."[21]

A published review of Smyth's speech stated that a country has a right to declare war against another because the "right of punishment . . . is little more than the right of self-defense, a right belonging alike to individuals and to States."[22] Smyth also stated that participation in the war against Mexico was a Christian duty. War was a necessary evil in our world and true Christians should support their country in war. "True patriotism . . . is, like true politeness, the offspring of piety."[23] The Methodist Episcopal Church, South (MECS) presented the same point of view in their 1851 Annual Report. Reflecting on the "success" of the war with Mexico, the report stated that "victory and conquest have ever followed the preaching of the cross."[24]

Destiny of the Southwest in Protestant Thought

Regardless of their position on the war, virtually all Protestants were in favor of American hegemony in the Southwest. Unitarian pastor A. P. Peabody lamented that "while the fortune of war hung in doubt, there were indeed many ready to denounce it. . . . But now that success has crowned our arms, we find many members and . . . leaders of that party joining in the congratulations and festivities that hail the recent victories."[25] Both during and immediately after the war with Mexico there was very little opposition to U.S. control over the Southwest. Even those who opposed territorial expansion during the hostilities saw it in a more favorable light once the land was conquered.[26]

Most nineteenth-century Protestant leaders seemed to agree with Josiah Strong, who stated in 1858 "that God, with infinite wisdom and skill, is training the Anglo-Saxon race for an hour sure to come in the world's future."[27] Even those who opposed the imperial expansion implicit in Manifest Destiny seemed to accept the idea that Anglo-Saxons had a special place in the world.[28] According to Livermore, a pacifist who opposed the war with Mexico, Anglo-Saxons "have the saving ideas of Science, Freedom, and Christianity, that are able, if diffused, to keep the life-blood flowing, in strong and pure tides through their own hearts, and also to stir the deep sleep of paganism with fresh and waking pulses of regeneration."[29]

Both pro-war and antiwar Protestant leaders held this view. Theodore Parker spoke vehemently against the war with Mexico, yet he described Mexico as "semibarbarous" and "miserable."[30] Sermons published by the American Home Missionary Society recorded this same sentiment. Eskine Mason preached that "the unmeasured superiority of Christian over unevangelized nations, is universally acknowledged."[31] An 1847 Society report contrasted the Pilgrims and Spaniards, drawing the conclusion that Protestants had a much more valuable civilization.[32] In 1848 a Society report stated that because of this superiority, American migration westward would produce "a vigorous and enterprising nation . . . furnished from the start with all the requisites for a state of high civilization."[33]

Several Protestant leaders saw the movements in the Southwest as part of a larger process involving the general advancement of Anglo-Saxons. Read, who condemned the Mexican-American War, stated that Anglo Americans were "planting the institutions of freedom, and displaying the improvements of civilization, and diffusing the benign influences of religion from the Atlantic to the Pacific."[34] According to Strong, the Anglo-Saxon had an "instinct or genius for colonizing . . . [and] pushing his way into new countries."[35] J. J. Miter told the American

Home Missionary Society that Anglo-Saxons in the New World would "not have fulfilled their noble destiny, until they have planted the . . . principles of the Reformation on the shore of the Pacific."[36] The Society also compared the "tent of the [westward] emigrant" to the "cabin of the May Flower" and asked "why may not other *Pilgrims* plant another *Plymouth* on the shore of the Pacific, with the germs of institutions, under whose benign operation their sons for ages, shall rejoice in *'Freedom to Worship God?'*"[37]

Even the Unitarian Morison took for granted that the United States would obtain more territories. He never argued for returning the Southwest to Mexico. His concern was that the West, and other future territorial additions, not be annexed as slave states or territories. He hoped Congress would pass a resolution "declaring the perpetual Independence from the tyranny of slavery, of all territories hereafter added to the United States."[38]

Most Protestants in the United States were convinced that God was working for and through them. Many compared themselves to the Israelites entering the land of Canaan. Richard Storrs told the American Home Missionary Society that "nations have been driven out before us, greater and mightier than we, that we might enter in, and take the land for an inheritance, as it is this day."[39]

Members of the Society saw their commission enlarging because "another of those great migrations that mark the history of the Anglo-Saxon race has begun."[40] According to Miter, this expansion from the Mississippi to the Pacific was inevitable, and "a few more swelling surges of emigration" would complete it.[41]

The only disagreement among Protestants had to do with explaining how God was moving in events such as the Mexican-American War and the subsequent migration into the Southwest. Most of those who opposed the war with Mexico favored U.S. expansion into the Southwest and saw it as part of

God's plan for Anglo-Saxons. Hart was merely concerned that the "conquest would be harmful to fulfilling the mission [of being an example to the world]."[42] Livermore stated that because Mexicans had been conquered, they would now very reluctantly adopt Anglo-Saxon "religious belief, social usages, forms of government, arts and sciences, and methods of governments, except by stern compulsion."[43] Instead of fighting a war, the United States should have negotiated with Mexico to secure "all the territory she wanted."[44] As a Protestant opposed to the war, Read attempted to explain God's work in history by concluding that God had used the Mexican-American War for good. Although war was wrong, "from the hour that the American flag floated over the City of Mexico, a new destiny awaited all those portions which were brought under Anglo-Saxon rule."[45] Those who favored the war spoke of it in much more glowing terms. According to the MECS 1851 Annual Report previously quoted, God working in the conquest of the Southwest was bringing His plan to fulfillment.[46]

A crucial part of God's plan for more religiously motivated Protestants with a missionary zeal included preaching the Protestant message. They were convinced that the United States had a special part in the expansion of Protestant faith. "America was now added to the known domains of the world, *to make room for the church*, and to become in its turn a fountain, from which should go forth streams of salvation to the ends of the earth."[47] Expansion of missionary activity into the Southwest formed part of the larger mission of bringing "other tribes and races under the obedience of God, and [in] harmony with his laws."[48]

Religiously motivated Protestants also had the associated goal of curtailing Catholicism. Hollis Read afterwards saw "the hand of God" in the fact that the war with Mexico had "inclosed vast territories within the domains of Protestantism, and thrown open to the influences of an evangelical Christianity and an Anglo-Saxon civilization a large Romish population."

He believed that the war was "nefarious," but God had used it to wrest away a once Roman Catholic territory "as the wants of the reformed religion have required" and placed it in Protestant control. Victory over Mexico provided an opportunity to cut back "the boundaries of Romanism."[49] The conquest of the Southwest opened the opportunity to extend Protestant faith to the Mexican Catholics who had never before been able to hear the Protestant message.

Protestants also felt that a part of their mission included extending the republican form of government in the Southwest and throughout the world. For some, preaching the Protestant gospel and promoting republicanism were part and parcel of their task. Baptist J. N. Granger thanked God because he was seeing the day "when this infant state of ours [will] give lessons in civil and religious liberty to the despotisms of the old world."[50] In his message to the American Home Missionary Society, Barnes referred to "the better influences of our Protestant and Republican institutions."[51] Read believed that God had given Anglo Americans the task of extending Protestantism and republicanism because they were a "progressive race." God had chosen people like the Puritans (and their descendants) for this task because they were "men who hated oppression, abhorred ignorance and vice—who were, in their very souls, *republicans* and *Christians*—these were the men, chosen out by sovereign Wisdom, to control the destinies of the new world."[52]

Protestant mission agencies also felt that they had a responsibility toward the people they had conquered. According to Livermore, the Mexicans of New Mexico and California were a "mongrel race" who had cheapened the "American birthright" by being given American citizenship.[53] These people had inherited "the cruelty, bigotry, and superstition that have marked the character of the Spaniards from the earliest times."[54] Therefore, Mexicans were doomed to "ignorance, degradation, and misery."[55] Episcopalian leader H. Forrester declared that Protestants had a responsibility to preach a message that could free and regenerate them by bringing them in contact "with American ideas and customs."[56]

Anglo-Saxons were a "strong race, which absorbs many others."[57] They needed to purify the Mexicans who were "indolent" and lacked "consistency" as a people.[58] Protestant missionaries would preach the gospel and extend their efforts to include "civilization, the introduction of the arts, and the establishment of good government among [the Mexicans]."[59] "A strong infusion of the American race would impart energy and industry gradually to the indolent Mexicans,"[60] as would the introduction into this "pagan" nation of a "Christian language" (English).[61] If Protestant missionaries were successful in converting the Mexicans into Protestants and good Americans they would fulfill an important part of their God-given task in the Southwest.

U.S. imperial expansion into the Southwest and Protestant support of that process created the framework for the Protestant evangelistic efforts among the conquered Mexicans. Victorious Protestants would proclaim the superiority of their faith to defeated Catholics and call them to become good U.S. citizens by accepting the Protestant faith. The takeover of the Southwest made conquest, and the need to adapt to it, an important component in the Mexican Catholic response to the Protestant message in the Southwest.

2

"Unfit for the Duties and Privileges of Citizens"

ANGLO AMERICAN PROTESTANT ATTITUDES
TOWARD THE MEXICANS OF THE SOUTHWEST

None but people advanced to a very high state of moral and intellectual improvement are capable, in a civilized state, of maintaining free government.
John C. Calhoun, "The Government of a White Race"
(1848)

[The New Mexicans are] not fond of work, but when it is absolutely necessary to buy candles and whiskey, and pay the musicians for a dance, you can rely on . . . [them] for working as long as the necessity lasts.
W. M. Thayer, "The New Mexican" (1890)

FROM AN ANGLO AMERICAN PROTESTANT PERSPECTIVE, THE CONquest of the Southwest was a mixed blessing. The United States had obtained land for expansion, but it now had the responsibility of dealing with three "exceptional populations"—Native

Americans, Mexican Americans and Mormons—the latter two of which were American citizens.[1] The latter presented a particular source of difficulties for the United States because these new citizens had a "foreign" language and religion. Anglo American Protestants viewed Mexican Americans as Catholic outsiders, who were unfit for the privileges of citizenship. Before going into the Southwest and meeting any Mexicans, Protestants already had a very negative view of the Mexican population. When they started moving into the area they saw no redeeming qualities in the Mexicans. The derogatory statements they made of the people demonstrate that they did not understand the religious, cultural, and social reality of the people. The missionaries' descriptions were often distorted and sometimes completely false. Nonetheless, by hearing their voices one understands what motivated them and why they were so surprised when their efforts did not produce the results they expected.

Strangers in Their Own Land[2]

The most telling Anglo American Protestant comment about the conquered Mexican Americans was that the new Anglo immigrant population labeled them as "foreigners." Though they were there when the Americans arrived, the conquest had changed their status. The conquerors failed to acknowledge that this group had lived on the land for several centuries and that the Spanish-speaking people were not the immigrants in the land. From the first time they came into contact with Mexican Americans, Protestant missionaries adopted this perspective. William C. Blair, a Presbyterian missionary to the Spanish-speaking in Texas when it was an independent republic (1836–1845), stated that "although this mission is for the present located in Texas, it is properly a mission to Mexico."[3]

This perspective became the established understanding after

the U.S. government gained control of the Southwest. Missionaries to the Mexican Americans in the 1870s described them as "foreign." In an 1872 letter, Thomas Harwood stated that ninety-six percent of the New Mexican population spoke a "foreign language (Spanish)." Throughout his many years of ministry, Harwood emphasized the "foreign character of the work . . . save the fact that it lies within the limits of our happy Republic."[4] Another Methodist worker in New Mexico called the Territory "the land of Montezuma."[5]

Because the Mexicans were "foreigners," Protestant missionaries and mission boards faced a dilemma. Since the Southwest was now a part of the United States, work among the people there, including the Spanish speaking, was the responsibility of denominational home mission boards. But these boards were not ready to take on this task. "Home missions" meant a focus on English-speaking Americans. "Different" peoples were the task of foreign mission boards—which officially had no jurisdiction in the United States.

Home mission boards responded differently to this dilemma. For example, PCUSA home mission agencies worked with the Spanish speaking though they considered that ministry "foreign" work. They hoped the day would come when Mexicans would be recognized as U.S. citizens, no longer "strangers or foreigners." They knew work among them would be difficult and the results slow because "the native population does not welcome us," and the Mexicans were strongly tied to Catholicism. Yet Protestants could not ignore these communities "and do nothing for their salvation." Progress and westward migration was making them more accessible, increasing the responsibility of Home Mission Boards.[6] The PCUSA home missions board wrote:

> We must begin the work among the Indians, the Mexicans and the Mormons, very much as we would in Persia or India; very much as foreign missionaries

> begin their work in foreign lands . . . we must begin
> among the children—open Schools and Sunday
> Schools, and through these expect to reach parents
> and the adult population, and with this new material
> at length build up Christian congregations, and pros-
> ecute the work of evangelization among the people.[7]

The MECS took the opposite approach. During the early years, their work among *tejanos* fell under the jurisdiction of the West Texas Conference. But in 1884 all Spanish-language ministry in Texas (and later Arizona) was placed under the foreign mission board. Spanish-language MECS congregations in the Southwest became part of conferences in Mexico, a situation that did not change until the early twentieth century.

However, deciding who was responsible for work among the Spanish-speaking people did not make the task any easier. Most Protestant missionaries and mission boards, whether under home or foreign mission boards, found that Anglo American Protestants could not get excited about work that was "neither foreign nor home." It was easier to find missionaries and raise funds for work in Mexico than for work among Mexican Americans in the Southwest. Protestant missionaries felt this ambivalence limited their evangelistic capabilities.[8]

Reasons for Rejecting the New Citizens

The Treaty of Guadalupe Hidalgo (1848) guaranteed American citizenship to all former Mexican citizens who chose to remain in the States. This created a dilemma for Anglo American Protestants. Some were fully convinced that non-Anglos could never be useful U.S. citizens. Others saw Mexican Americans as a people who could eventually be made good citizens, but only with a great deal of work.[9]

For those convinced that Mexican Americans could never be good U.S. citizens, race was a chief concern. According to most Anglo Americans, only "white" people were capable of self-government. They discounted the potential of Spanish-speaking people because they were mixed race. There was "good" Spanish blood in them, but it was mixed with Indian blood. According to Senator Calhoun, one of the major mistakes made by the Spanish in America was "placing these colored races [indigenous peoples and mestizos] on an equality with the white race." Not all peoples could maintain civil and religious liberty. "None but people advanced to a very high state of moral and intellectual improvement are capable, in a civilized state, of maintaining free government."[10] Yet the view of Mexican Americans as non-white was often applied inconsistently. In many places Anglos differentiated between "pure" Spanish and "mixed bloods," usually based on both skin color and economic standing. For example, Anglos often called the Spanish-speaking elite "white," where Anglos were a minority and wanted the support of the *ricos* to maintain control over the "cholos" or mestizos (of Spanish and Indian descent).[11]

Anglo American Protestants were also concerned about the perceived "Catholic threat." They considered Mexican Americans particularly problematic because they were mixed race, spoke a different language, were American citizens, *and* were devoted Catholics. If Mexican American Catholics were to join with other American Catholics who were already citizens they could wreak havoc on the "American way of life" and the institutions of liberty held dear by Protestant America.

Those who opposed U.S. citizenship for Mexican Americans argued that it cheapened the value of being an "American." They wanted to limit citizenship to Anglo Protestants— the only ones who could be "good Americans." This view was not held by merely fringe elements in American society; it was the dominant opinion of the day. Even Livermore, who strongly opposed the war with Mexico, maintained a similar perspective.[12]

Americanization of the New Citizens

When the Mexican Americans became U.S. citizens, many Protestants considered the task of Americanizing them indispensible. Mexican Americans had never received the tools necessary for becoming "law-abiding, industrious and thrifty citizens" of the United States.[13] They were now members of the "national family," yet in their current state, they were still "unfit for the duties and privileges of citizens."[14] The goal was to make Mexican Americans "American citizens such as will bless the land."[15] According to MEC missionary David Moore

> the necessity of making good citizens out of the Mexicans who have become an integrate part of our nations, would be sufficient even without the higher Gospel motives, to cause benefaction to that end to flow in deep and constant streams.[16]

If Spanish-speaking people were to become good citizens, the missionaries were convinced that they needed to help them correct many things. According to the missionaries Mexicans did not have "the spirit of progress" that motivated the North American.[17] They also needed to adopt Anglo American technological advances and eating and dressing habits—then they would be able to enjoy "more of the comforts of civilized life."[18] Mexican Americans also needed to become "moral and upright men and women, with cultured minds and upright principles"[19] by removing "popular superstition and ignorance."[20] It was also indispensable that they learn English.[21] Not only were American Protestants convinced that Mexican Americans needed to make these changes, they also believed that they wanted such changes for themselves and their children.[22]

Anglo American Protestants interested in helping Mexican Americans become good citizens linked this task to evangelistic and educational efforts. Protestant missionaries wanted them to form good Christian (Protestant) homes where the Bible was read, people prayed and praised God, and the Sabbath was kept.[23] According to Thomas Harwood, missionaries needed to evangelize Mexican Americans by educating them in American schools.[24] Education and evangelization were almost synonymous terms for the missionary teachers sent to start schools in northern New Mexico.[25] They believed that the Protestant educational process would help Mexican Americans realize that they were being enslaved by the Catholic priesthood and would show them the importance of becoming "more enlightened and civilized."[26] It would also remove the prejudices of the people toward an Anglo American style of education[27] and prepare the Spanish speaking (particularly of New Mexico) for the task of becoming citizens of a state in the Union.[28]

Anglo Protestant Assumptions about the Mexican American Population

Most Anglo American Protestants held the general assumption that Mexican Americans were morally degenerate. A fellow Anglo American informed Melinda Rankin, one of the first Protestant missionaries in Texas after 1848, that "stealing was inherent among those people, and could not be eradicated." She assumed the first part of the statement to be true, but found that they could learn to abandon the practice.[29] Alexander Darley, a Presbyterian missionary in southern Colorado, stated that

> they [Mexican Americans] are a very degraded people, in many respects. They think a violation of the seventh commandment is bad before marriage, but not afterwards. They think that a thing is not wrong unless found out. That is one of the strongest elements of the Mexican character too often.[30]

The missionaries also considered Mexican Americans "mentally weak," unable to think for themselves, because their religion had never encouraged intellectual activity.[31] They lived in a "sorrowful state of ignorance" in which only a few men were educated, and practically no women could even read Spanish. From the missionaries' perspective, the "Mexicans" were at the mental level of children, since only thirty percent could read and write.[32] The responsibility for this situation was laid directly at the feet of the Catholic Church. According to the Protestants the priests had no interest in seeing the people advance with the help of Protestant missions and schools; they were convinced that Catholic priests wanted to keep their people illiterate.[33]

This distorted view of Mexican Americans affected how Protestant missionaries understood their work. A BGC missionary in Texas described *tejano* Baptist ministers as "pitifully illiterate, ministering to a membership of some two hundred of the most illiterate poor people."[34] A Methodist in New Mexico admitted that working in Spanish-speaking communities did not "require that degree of native and acquired ability that is required of those engaged in religious work among the more highly cultured classes."[35]

Anglo American Protestants also described Mexican Americans as lazy. *Neomejicanos* were "slow and quaint, primitive and picturesque in spite of [themselves], with a Rip Van Winkle air, as one taken by surprise—just awaking from a dreamy siesta. To the active, nervous, ambitious American, he seems out of date, a relic of a past age."[36] Closely related to this laziness was a "lack of initiative" which put them in tension with Americans. This passivity was not necessarily due to an inherent inability, "for in their veins ran the blood of the greatest pioneers the world has ever known." Instead, Protestants attributed the Mexican American lack of initiative to Roman Catholicism, "a system of intellectual and spiritual servitude that crushed the individual mind and aspirations."[37]

According to American Protestants, this laziness created dependency in the Mexican population. "Mexicans" lacked "firmness and strength of purpose." This made it difficult for missionaries to organize strong churches among them, because "they require constant training and support. Their churches fall easily into disorder, and need constant encouragement."[38] Mexican Americans were also economically dependent. Too many were "living off the charity of Christians who have to practice self-denial in order to help the idle and thriftless."[39] The missionaries needed to teach them self-reliance.

The missionaries linked this perceived lethargy to cultural inferiority. Anglo Americans were coming face to face with a people who had "fallen behind" while "the march of civilization had taken grand strides, almost everywhere else." From their perspective, the reason for this was that Spanish-speaking communities had no "Bibles, schools [or] proper instruction."[40] Mexican American customs "proved" their culture's inferiority to the missionaries. They lived in very primitive dwellings with only rudimentary furniture. Their homes were filthy and they ate on the ground, often surrounded by "hungry dogs and naked children."[41]

Anglos also considered Mexican Americans primitive technologically. For example, their agricultural methods had not changed for hundreds of years.[42] Thomas Harwood, an early Protestant missionary in New Mexico, noted in 1870 that the few bridges or public roads in the territory had been built by the government or Protestant pioneers, and "hardly an American plow, wagon or buggy could be found" in New Mexico.[43] He was convinced that the region needed railroad steam whistles "to break the silence of a slumbering people."[44]

This negative analysis all tied back, in the missionaries' understanding, to the fact that Mexican Americans were Catholics and that the vast majority remained Catholic even after they heard the Protestant message. The missionaries saw Catholicism at the heart of all of the other problems faced by Mexican Americans, including illiteracy, ignorance, and irreligion.[45] It had "fettered the intellect" of the Spanish-speaking people.[46] They were "the most bigoted Papists—as bigoted as they are ignorant," who lived in "a most benighted condition."[47] According to the missionaries the Catholicism practiced by Mexican Americans in the Southwest was not really a form of Christianity. It encouraged idolatry, extensive use of money on feast days, and in New Mexico, invited people to beat "themselves during Lent to atone for their sins."[48] Catholicism had made New Mexico

> one of the darkest corners of the world. As if the clouds of the dark ages, receding from the eastern skies of infallible Romanism growing thicker and darker in their flight, had culminated over the intellectual skies of the Mexican people and drenched their soil with the polluting floods of Jesuitical traditions, superstitions and ignorance.[49]

Furthermore, Protestant missionaries felt that the new priests sent into the Southwest by the U.S. Catholic Church were not helping the people change. They continued the practices of demanding excessive tithes and charging exorbitant prices for baptisms, the Eucharist, and other so-called sacraments (e.g., marriages, extreme unction and prayers for the dead at extortionate prices).[50]

Protestants accused the Catholic hierarchy of keeping the Bible out of the people's reach and attempting to maintain their bondage to "the dreadful tyranny of papal laws." To work among Mexican Americans was to enter "the enemy's camp." According to Melinda Rankin, one of the earliest Protestant missionaries, giving out Bibles was like shooting missiles into Satan's territory. The few she was able to place in the hands of Spanish-speaking people had done "essential damage . . . in this kingdom of darkness, where Satan had so long reigned with undisputed sway."[51]

From a Protestant perspective, Catholicism was also the cause of physical poverty among Mexican Americans. The "awful condition of the Mexican, who traverses our own Texas plains" was directly attributed to the control of the Catholic Church. Yet, concluded the Blanco Baptist Association (BGC), because of the Mexicans' "former deeds of treachery" against the United States, there was "no eye to pity him, no God to save." Their actions had "closed the doors of charity against him, and therefore we take no notice of him or his wants."[52]

Based on this very skewed analysis of the Mexican population, Protestant missionaries went into the Southwest convinced of the importance of their mission. Theirs was a continuation of the battle between Protestantism and Catholicism and Protestantism had to win. Their task seemed clear and the motivations for it right. The conquered Mexicans were a people with no hope for a future in the U.S. Southwest unless they Americanized and became Protestants. Once the missionaries started preaching they believed the Mexicans would soon recognize this reality and readily accept Protestantism.

Because of this perspective the missionaries did not have the tools to recognize the distortions and fallacies in their understanding of the Spanish speaking. Once they began work in the Southwest any lack of "success" would be blamed on the Mexican population and the Catholic Church. It would not be until the twentieth century when some Protestant missionaries would begin to question whether their initial analysis might have been wrong.[53]

3

"Making Good Citizens Out of the Mexicans"

MOTIVATIONS FOR PROTESTANT MISSION WORK AMONG MEXICAN AMERICANS

*We hold the key to Mexico's evangelization and to the re-
demption of the whole Southwestern frontier of the United
States . . . [because] Methodism appears first on the field
in most of this territory.*

Texas Christian Advocate (1885)

*The work of educating these people in the knowledge of
Christ Jesus is a great work. The Spanish speaking people
know more about saints and images than they know about
Christ. Nothing but the Spirit of God can lead them to see
that God is to be worshipped without an image, and that
they can pray to Christ without the aid of a saint.*

John Menaul (1891)

*[P]atriotism and home missions are inseparably united.
Neither can stand, in the mind of the Christian citizen,
without the other.*

Sherman H. Doyle (1905)

THE PREVIOUS CHAPTER DESCRIBED THE "PROBLEM" AS PERCEIVED
by American Protestant mission agencies: Mexican Catholics
had been accepted as U.S. citizens and these people were not fit
for the privilege. This situation served, in turn, as the chief mo-
tivator for Protestant mission work among the Mexicans of the
Southwest. The Mexican population needed to hear the Protestant message to be freed from Catholicism. Closely tied to this
message was Anglo American culture, perceived by Protestant
leaders to be the logical result of living out the Protestant message. To preach a Protestant understanding of the gospel was
also to promote the best of Anglo American cultural, social, political, and economic values. Both theological and cultural un-
derstandings of Anglo American Protestantism motivated missionaries to evangelize Mexican American Catholics.

Doubts about Evangelizing Mexican Americans

The rhetoric used to justify the conquest of the Southwest did
not translate into a strong missionary enterprise, however.
Many Protestants questioned whether there should even be a
missionary effort among the Mexican American population.
Many home missions leaders were convinced that mission agencies should focus their energies on the Anglo American immigrants entering the newly conquered Southwest. When Melinda
Rankin visited churches in the eastern United States to raise
funds for her missionary efforts in Texas, she found that many
Protestant leaders and members were not interested in reaching
the Mexican American population. She reported that "the prejudices existing against the Mexicans, engendered during the
late war, often proved great barriers to my success." One Presbyterian leader told her that "the Mexicans were a people just
fit to be exterminated from the earth." Another person, a Presbyterian minister, even stated, "We had better send bullets and
gunpowder to Mexico than Bibles."[1]

Nonetheless, Protestant mission agencies did send out a few missionaries to work among Mexican Americans during the 1850s. The MEC and MECS sent missionaries to New Mexico and Texas, respectively. Northern (American) Baptists entered New Mexico, and Melinda Rankin represented the PCUSA in Texas (though she was not officially sent by any mission agency). John McCullough, another Presbyterian missionary, also worked in San Antonio for a short period. The American Bible Society sent a colporteur, Robert Thompson, to distribute Spanish Bibles and Testaments in south Texas. These initial efforts were mostly short lived and produced few long term results, apart from two small congregations in Peralta and Socorro, New Mexico, and a few *tejanos* who joined the MECS congregation in Corpus Christi, Texas. These initial lackluster results caused some Protestant leaders to question whether there was any possibility of missionary success among "such a hopeless race" as the Mexican.[2]

Another reason that Protestant mission leaders questioned whether their mission agencies should work among the Mexican population was that the conquest of the Southwest opened large amounts of new land to settlers from the eastern United States and Europe. Anglo Americans and Northern Europeans had been migrating into Texas since the 1820s, and the Gold Rush of 1849 caused rapid migration into California. By 1850 Anglo Americans and European immigrants represented the overwhelming majority of the population in northern California.[3] People were also migrating into other regions of the Southwest. This migration accelerated after railroads penetrated the region in the early 1880s. These new settlers had many spiritual needs, and home mission societies felt it was important to send workers among them. New communities lacked churches, and children were growing up with little or no religious instruction. There was a strong desire to reach out to these "white" settlers. This desire limited interest in reaching the Spanish-speaking population.[4] Mission boards and many individuals recognized the importance of preaching the gospel to the "Mexicans," but

> to train the American children in our midst—those who have come from our eastern homes, who are our own flesh and blood—is an even greater responsibility and as grand a calling. Without our New West schools, scores, yes, hundreds, of eager children would not have any means of education save those afforded by the few schools of the sisters, nuns, and monks of the Roman church.[5]

Motives for Mission

Although many Anglo American Protestants were indifferent, and efforts before the Civil War yielded limited success, some felt a strong motivation to work among Mexican Americans in the Southwest. A review of the literature produced by Protestant missionary societies during the nineteenth century and the missionaries' own writings reveal a broad range of motives for ministry among Mexican Americans.

The Gospel Mandate

Since the Protestant missionaries were convinced that Mexican American Catholics were not "fully" Christian, they often mentioned preaching the gospel so that people could be saved from their sins, and other biblical themes related to Jesus' Great Commission of making disciples of all nations (Matthew 28:18–20) when referring to the need to reach Mexican Americans in the Southwest. Many early missionaries and some mission agencies made direct or indirect references to this biblical mandate in their writings. The BGC of Texas made the most references to Jesus' evangelistic mandate in relationship to Mexican Americans in the Southwest. At least eight different references to the Great Commission appear in various BGC reports. Within the BGC, the Blanco Baptist Association, an association of Baptist churches in south Texas, is the group that most often mentions the biblical mandate as the reason for preaching the gospel in the Spanish language. The association's "Mexican and Colored Population Committee" reports of 1880, 1881, 1882, 1890, and 1895 all refer to the gospel, Christ's mandate, or non-Christians' need of salvation.

> All that is necessary . . . is to give them the Gospel in their own language,[6]

> It devolved upon us in a great measure as a denomination to teach them how to obey these great commands, that we should avail ourselves of every opportunity to instruct them and render them all the assistance we can.[7]

> Just now is a more favorable time to effect good in the name of Jesus among the Mexicans than any time in the past.[8]

> May the God of heaven in His own good time, may that time be soon, devise some means by which these perishing thousands shall be brought to Christ. Let us reward them for all their mistakes of the past by giving them the Gospel of the Son of God.[9]

> They [tejanos] are here at our doors, and that they have souls to be saved or to be lost admits of no doubt.[10]

Despite this rhetoric, the churches of the Blanco Association did not make a serious commitment to work among Mexican Americans during the nineteenth century. An 1881 report mentions work in Laredo, but no other documents of the period make reference to Spanish-language ministries in that city until the following decade. An 1895 report laments that "what to do with the Mexicans in our midst is a problem that has vexed our Baptist brotherhood for the past years."[11]

The annual reports of the Baptist General Association of Texas likewise make at least three references to the Great Com-

mission mandate. They relate specifically to reports of the work
that began among *tejanos* in San Antonio in 1887. The reports
describe the work there and in other parts of Texas in light of
God's call, highlighting the opportunity for Texas Baptists to
reach *tejanos* with the gospel.

> God hath set before us an open door in this work and
> we have entered and have been blessed.[12]

> God has opened to us the door of their hearts and the
> work done among them has been graciously blessed.[13]

> We have also some very needy fields among our
> Mexican population elsewhere in the state. . . . We
> ought to heed their Macedonian cries.[14]

The first two long-term Presbyterian missionaries among *tejanos*, Melinda Rankin and Walter Scott, refer to the biblical
mandate to persuade Presbyterians to support their ministry. In
her book *Texas in 1850*, Melinda Rankin attempts to convince
New England Presbyterians of the need to send workers to
Texas. She quotes Jesus' statement about leaving all for the
kingdom of God and contrasts the eternal value of reaching *tejanos* for Christ with the earthly treasures being sought in the
mines of California and Mexico: "Are there not Christians to
be found among the highly favored portions of our country,
who can be influenced by such heaven-born principles, to come
out upon that mission of mercy which brought the Son of God
from the bosom of his Father?"[15]

More than thirty years after Rankin, Walter Scott began his
ministry in the San Marcos, Texas, area. As he sought to challenge the PCUS to minister to *tejanos* he stated:

> It is for us, as a people charged with the high com-
> mission to evangelize the world, to meet it calmly
> and resolutely and discharge our Christian obliga-
> tion. . . . We have seen too many instances of the ef-
> ficacy of the precious word of God and of the work
> of the Holy Spirit among them to doubt for a mo-

ment their need of the Gospel and our duty to give it
to them.[16]

Many other Protestant missionaries alluded to Jesus' call
when trying to convince people to support their work. Matilda
Allison, a Presbyterian teacher in New Mexico, quotes Jesus'
words "the field now seems ripe for the harvest" (John 4:35)
when referring to work among *neomejicanos*.[17] Methodists in
California also made indirect allusions to a divine mandate in
relationship to *californios*: "To neglect this field longer is ren-
dering us liable of incurring the Divine displeasure."[18] And a report in the minutes of the (Southern) California Conference sees
God's hand as "clearly providential" in initial efforts to reach
californios in Los Angeles.[19]

The Importance of Reaching Mexico

Another motivation for working among Mexican Americans in
the Southwest was their potential as a bridge to reach Mexico
with the Protestant message. At the time of the U.S. takeover of
the Southwest the Mexican government did not allow Protestant missionaries to enter Mexico. Therefore, some missionaries saw work among Mexican Americans not as an end in itself
but as a means of making contact with people from Mexico, indirectly influencing the Mexican population, and practicing
evangelistic skills among Mexican Americans until there was
freedom to preach in Mexico. Many Protestant missionaries in
Texas had this perspective. Though Mexico remained closed,
south Texas provided a better opportunity for preaching to the
Spanish-speaking population than had ever existed before the
U.S. takeover of the Southwest.

When Texas became an independent country in 1836, Old
School Presbyterians sent two missionaries, Sumner Bacon and
William Blair, to work among the Mexicans there. Due to the
unstable situation (e.g., Mexican attempts to reconquer the ter-

ritory and Indian attacks) neither spent much time working among the Spanish-speaking people. Both of them considered their work in Texas to be temporary. They went to the Republic of Texas to learn Spanish and to wait for an opportunity to enter Mexico. They "saw their activity in Texas as provisional and secondary to missionary endeavors in Mexico itself."[20]

The first Protestant missionary in south Texas, Melinda Rankin, went to Brownsville after the end of the Mexican-American War (1848) to reach the people of Mexico. She continued working in Texas until the Mexican government allowed Protestant missionaries to enter the country. Her book, *Texas in 1850*, describes the need in Texas but also refers to the opportunities the location provided for reaching Mexico. Her desire in writing the book was "to enlist Christian sympathy and cooperation in aid of evangelizing a country [Texas] which is destined, evidently, to exert an important influence over other contiguous countries [Mexico]."[21] Rankin saw that Brownsville had extensive ties with various parts of Mexico. Because of this, she felt that the city should be "regarded an important medium of communication by which Protestantism may be introduced into Mexico, and hence appears the necessity of a strong influence of that sort being concentrated at this point." Rankin also considered that the border communities of Roma, Rio Grande, Laredo, and El Paso were important locations that should be "secured with strong Bible influences" so that the (Protestant version of the) gospel could enter Mexico.[22]

Rankin was particularly interested in the indirect effect that evangelizing *tejanos* would have on Mexico. When she arrived in Brownsville in 1850 she focused on ways of indirectly influencing Mexico from the U.S. side of the border. She believed that if Texas could be elevated to a "high point of moral power and efficiency," it would have a positive influence in "the moral elevation of degraded Mexico." According to Rankin, Texas needed the efforts of Protestant missionaries because of the destitution of its own people, Spanish-speaking and otherwise. But the missionaries were also necessary because Providence had pointed out "Texas as an agent to operate upon the Papal power in Mexico."[23]

The relationship between reaching *tejanos* in southwest Texas and the evangelization of Mexico was also an important consideration for the Blanco Baptist Association. They recognized the importance of reaching the Mexican Americans of their area because it "would be an important step toward evangelizing the border states of Mexico."[24] If there were enough money to support missionaries there might soon be Baptist churches among *tejanos*, which "would honor and advance the cause of truth even beyond our borders."[25]

Presbyterians in Texas viewed their ministry among Mexican Americans in the same light. The first Presbyterian Church formed in San Antonio in the 1840s transmitted the following resolution to its Foreign (Mission) Board:

> Whereas the town of San Antonio, in Western Texas, contains a population of more than two thousand Mexicans, and whereas this town carries on considerable trade with Eastern Mexico and affords facilities for distributing Bibles, etc., among that deluded people, Therefore, Resolved that, should Texas be transferred to the Domestic Board, that town be recommended to the Foreign Board to be continued under their care as a suitable station for operating upon the population there and also for introducing the gospel into Mexico.[26]

Walter Scott, called the "Father of Spanish-speaking Presbyterianism" in Texas, approached ministry among the Spanish-speaking communities of that state from a similar perspective. For him, the presbytery of western Texas had "no western boundary—it can take in the entire republic of Mexico." Because of the constant comings and goings of Mexicans across the international border, evangelizing both *tejanos* and Mexi-

can immigrants in Texas contributed indirectly to the evangelization of Mexico. According to Scott, "the Gospel leaven is
being carried to their native land where it has borne fruit in a
number of instances."[27]

A Response to Roman Catholicism

As mentioned earlier, what most preoccupied Protestant missionaries among Mexican Americans was Roman Catholicism,
a major concern of all Protestant denominations during the
nineteenth century. They saw Catholicism as a direct threat to
Protestant America. Protestants were afraid that the Roman
Catholic Church would gain control of U.S. institutions
through the growing influence of Catholic immigrants from Europe. Protestants needed to convert Catholics in the U.S. because the Catholic Church was sending missionaries to convert
North American Protestants. If Catholics were ever to become
a majority in the United States, the Protestants believed that the
results would be disastrous for the Anglo American way of life
and the institutions of liberty held dear by Protestant America.[28]
Making the Mexicans of the Southwest U.S. citizens only exas-
perated the situation.[29]

Home Mission Monthly, a Presbyterian magazine, was one
of the home mission periodicals most concerned with the perceived threat posed by Roman Catholicism in the United States.
When it reported on the work among Mexicans in the Southwest it usually referred to the dangers of a Catholic majority in
New Mexico as one of the reasons for Protestant missionary efforts. Missionary reports often focused on the negative effects
of Catholicism on the Mexican American population. Editorial
comments often pressed the issue beyond the specifics in New
Mexico to the perceived dangers to all of the United States.[30]

Many Protestant leaders feared that, if their missionary efforts failed, a Roman Catholic majority would vote to destroy

democratic American institutions. To "prove" their point, missionaries to New Mexico reminded their supporters that Bishop Lamy of Santa Fe was French and that he had brought many French priests into the diocese. They claimed that the diocese in Santa Fe was pervaded with a "spirit foreign to American views." These priests there were "not in sympathy with republican ideas and institutions, and are bold in their opposition to them."[31] Because they were foreigners, the priests did not see the need to obey the laws of the [32]United States and seemed to encourage *neomejicanos* not to obey them.[33] And as late as the beginning of the twentieth century, Emily Harwood, a pioneer Methodist worker in New Mexico, still had her doubts about whether Congress should admit New Mexico as a state in the Union. She was concerned that the Jesuits might be able to gain control of the state government and "overthrow our free American institutions."[34]

Protestant missionaries also wanted to convert people from Catholicism because they were sure that it kept Mexican Americans under spiritual bondage and turned them away from the true gospel. A common adjective used by many missionaries and mission agencies in reference to the Spanish-speaking people of the Southwest was "superstitious." They were not only "in a state of unregeneracy, but [they] are also trammeled with many superstitions."[35] When the missionaries spoke of superstitious practices they were most often referring to the Mexican American Catholic religious devotion to the Virgin Mary and the saints. Several published articles describe the "Romish superstitions" and "idol" worship of the Spanish-speaking population. Most Protestant missionaries shared Walter Scott's perspective that

> they [the Mexicans] do not pray; they do not come unto God by Christ; they know not the joy of drawing near with boldness unto a throne of grace. They have a pagan's idea of sin and repentance; they know

nothing of regeneration, nor of the indispensable work of the Spirit. In a word, they are without God, and without hope in the world.[36]

Protestant missionaries also described Roman Catholicism as a dead faith; it could not lead Mexican Americans toward a vibrant personal relationship with Jesus Christ. Its teachings and worship were empty, and many Mexicans were "crying out for the Living Bread,"[37] something they would find only in the Protestant message. Therefore, the missionaries did not see their work in the Southwest as proselytizing. They were drawing people away from a dead religion to a living faith.

Spiritual bondage was another common theme. Mexican American Catholics were "shut up in the prison-house of papal power"[38] that controlled every area of their lives and kept them from understanding their situation. Though there were few Catholic priests in the region, Protestant missionaries were convinced that Mexican Americans in the Southwest were "oppressed and priest-ridden"[39] "as much as in Mexico, or Spain, or South America."[40] It was the priests' job to keep the people in ignorance so that they would blindly accept the Vatican's instructions.

Specifically, the missionaries claimed that the priests prohibited the people from reading the Bible or the tracts given to them by the Protestant missionaries.[41] A Congregational missionary reported that the priests told the people, "you have no power to read the Bible. It belongs to the priests. If one of you read it, you cannot understand, because you are ignorants [sic], and besides that your church does not allow you to read it."[42] The priests also attempted to control what was taught in the public schools where Catholics were a majority. They did not want the people to have access to an education that might open their minds to the falseness of Catholicism. This created a situation where "little is taught in these [public] schools [controlled by Catholics] except prayers, and the superstition of the Romish Church."[43]

Priestly control was so complete that the people were not even able to discern that they needed the Protestant gospel. They were "intensely bigoted" against the Protestant message.[44]

Since Protestant missionaries were convinced of the superiority of their message and the potential effectiveness of their strategy, the Mexican Americans' lack of response to their message could only be explained by the Catholic Church's control over them. The Catholic hierarchy adversely affected Protestant mission work in several ways. First, it claimed an "exclusive right to teach and guard the oracles of God" and prohibited Catholics from even listening to the Protestant message.[45] Most Mexican Americans heeded their warning. Second, Catholic priests often actively opposed Protestant missionary teachers who attempted to start village (plaza) schools in areas of New Mexico where there was no public education.[46] The schools were a part of the larger Protestant mission strategy, although the missionaries presented them as opportunities for all children to gain an education. The priests suspected proselytism and, to the chagrin of the missionary teachers, often prohibited parents from sending their children to these schools.

Another common adjective used by the Protestant missionaries to describe Mexican Americans in the Southwest was "degraded." The missionaries believed that the Roman Catholic religious system not only deceived the Spanish-speaking population but also encouraged them to live in a degraded condition. In their eyes, the Church encouraged the people to practice vices, such as drinking and dancing during feast day celebrations, because it used them as a means of raising money for the Church. The priests were inducing the people "to follow the road of error and vice, themselves being the principal actors in the labyrinth of iniquity."[47]

The Protestant missionaries also claimed that because of the lack of proper teaching by the priests, adultery was openly practiced in Mexican American communities and was not con-

sidered wrong "unless found out."[48] Many families began "with
no marriage at all."[49] Missionaries also reported that some
Mexican American priests had mistresses at the time of the
American takeover (1848). Because the Church encouraged
vice, and its leaders did not provide good examples, it could not
call the people to a higher moral standard.

Missionaries reported that the Church also robbed the
people of "all progress and enterprise attendant upon diligent
labor."[50] Mexican Americans could not advance socially or economically because of the demands placed on them by the
Catholic religious system. Priests charged for all their services,
including masses, prayers, and bell ringing. They even charged
extra at weddings if the couple wanted to enter through the
front door. Not only did they charge for their services, they
forced the people to use their services, for example, by not al-
lowing them to bury unbaptized children in consecrated
ground.[51] Services were not cheap. "It often requires a year's
earnings to have a priest present at a burial of their dead."[52]

Protestant missionaries in New Mexico often focused on a
specific Catholic lay society, the *Penitentes*. They were a religious penitential society that had existed in New Mexico for
several centuries. They served an important religious and social
function during the Spanish and Mexican periods because there
were few priests in the region. But the Catholic hierarchy, both
in the Mexican and American periods, tried to curtail their
practices because of their penitential practices. By the time of
the U.S. takeover of the Southwest they had gone underground.
Penitentes practiced various forms of physical penitence during
Holy Week, including floggings, cutting, and, occasionally, cru-
cifixions. Most *neomejicanos* did not practice these rituals and
few missionaries ever actually saw much of what the *Penitentes*
did. Nonetheless, Protestant missionaries described these peni-
tent practices to prove that *neomejicano* Catholicism was essentially pagan and superstitious. Many missionaries in New Mex-

ico considered these penitential practices the epitome of the enslaving practices of Mexican American Catholicism.[53]

Protestant missionaries were overjoyed whenever a Mexican American left Catholic "enslavement" and became a Protestant. The 1886 Annual report of the Congregational Church in New Mexico and Arizona describes the people's joy as three early *neomejicano* converts accepted baptism. "Tears were in many eyes as three of these brown sons and daughters of New Mexico, brought up in the thralldom of Romanism, bowed to receive the ordinance of baptism, not being satisfied with the Romish rite."[54] The joy of the missionaries was confident because Mexican Americans who had been freed from the spiritual bondage of the Catholic Church "seldom go back to Romanism."[55]

Demonstrating the Superiority of Protestantism

Connected with the motive of counteracting the Catholic Church, many early missionaries wanted to prove that Protestantism was a superior form of Christianity. The issue was not merely doctrinal; they felt it was crucial to show that Protestantism produced a better society and economic order. Catholicism kept the people tied to a semi-pagan religion. The Protestant Church offered people freedom from that religious thralldom. Protestantism also gave them the opportunity to worship God according to the dictates of their own conscience. The intelligent portion of the Spanish-speaking population would be able to see the difference between the two and would be drawn to the Protestant faith.[56]

The missionary also strove to demonstrate the superiority of Protestantism in the area of morality. Protestantism, they taught, encouraged a personal moral code far superior to that taught and practiced by Catholicism. Moral superiority, Protestants believed, would also help further the gospel in Mexico. A strong faith and morality developed along the border would produce

such a contrast with the practices of the Mexican population
that it would clearly demonstrate the superiority of Protestantism over Catholicism. The result would be to "constrain the degraded Mexicans to yield to the influence of that system of faith,
which might elevate them to the like happy condition."[57]

Another way to show the "superiority" of Protestantism
over Catholicism was by comparing the technological advances
of American and Mexican American societies. Protestants considered Mexican Americans very primitive. Under Roman
Catholic control they had not made the technological advance-
ments that would have been possible under a system that encouraged free expression such as Protestantism, which now, the
missionaries believed, was changing all of that. Protestant
churches and mission schools were encouraging people to learn
to use technology brought by American Protestant civilization.
Although Mexican Americans tended to be reluctant, they
slowly began to adopt North American tools, modes of con-
struction, dress, and food. They now had more of the comforts
of civilized life than their ancestors ever had.[58] The missionary
pointed to these changes with pride.

From the perspective of the missionaries, Protestantism was
also superior as a facilitator of literacy and education. When
Protestant missionaries first entered the Southwest they found
"gross illiteracy, debasing immorality, and a low plane of intellectual development." Few of the people could write, and the
Catholic Church worked hard to keep education from "spreading its enlightening influence" over the people.[59] Despite
Catholic opposition, Protestants developed public and private
schools where people could learn and enjoy the benefits of the
technologically advanced and enlightened Protestant civilization. Slowly, the Catholic population seemed to recognize the
superiority of the Protestant schools—whether private or "public."[60] Missionaries were glad to see that Mexican Americans
who became Protestants fared even better than Spanish-

speaking Catholics educated in Protestant or public schools. A representative of the home mission board of the MEC reported that in Peralta, New Mexico, the first community where the Methodists started a church,

> The larger portion of the people are Protestants, and over seventy of these are members of our Church. They are by far the most cultivated of the town. Their superiority is seen in their general appearance, in their home comforts, and in their evident intelligence. Books and papers are seen in every one of their homes.[61]

Denominational Rivalry

All early Protestant missionaries found a common enemy in Roman Catholicism. But the missionaries of the various denominational groups were also motivated by the challenge to prove the superiority of their particular form of Protestantism. Although denominational rivalry was never an overt issue, it occasionally showed up in various writings. Baptist leaders and missionaries in particular often mentioned the superiority of their doctrine as a reason for ministry among the Spanish-speaking population. Two pre-Civil War Baptist missionaries to New Mexico, Hiram Read and Lewis Smith, were convinced that their denomination's teaching transcended all others. Smith was convinced that only the Baptists could provide a clear religious alternative to Catholic hegemony in New Mexico.

Baptists in Texas used similar reasoning to motivate their denomination to reach out to *tejanos*. An 1880 report on the "Colored and Spanish-speaking Population" to the Blanco Baptist Association includes a description of MECS work in the region. The committee chair was convinced that because many Methodist converts were "Baptist in principle, and would unite with us if an opportunity were offered," a Baptist missionary should be sent to them as soon as possible.[62] An 1894 report to the Association once again refers to what the Methodists were doing: "The Methodists have been very energetic in this matter, and I think we could accomplish much if we would only try."[63]

Emily Harwood (MEC) made several references to Presbyterian work in the area of education in New Mexico. She often compared Methodist and Presbyterian efforts, recognizing that the latter had done more. Nonetheless, she made it clear that the reason for the latter's success was that Presbyterians had better funding. If the Methodist missionaries had received the same amount of support, she ventured, they would have been equally successful.[64] Presbyterian George Darley, a missionary in southern Colorado, wrote that each presbytery wanted to have home mission ground on which to work because each wanted to participate in "the conquest of the border land for God and Presbyterianism."[65]

Americanization and the American Mandate

Another motivation for preaching to Mexican Americans in the Southwest had to do with the responsibility conferred on Anglo Americans by conquering Mexican Americans. Anglo Americans, considering themselves a superior race, felt a responsibility toward more "backwards" peoples, particularly those whom they were displacing. Melinda Rankin felt that Anglo Americans should commiserate with "the helpless condition of these perishing millions of souls [Mexicans in the Southwest and Mexico] under the iron heel of papal power, with all its soul-destroying influences." The United States had "conquered them and subjugated them to its own terms." Americans could not ignore the plight of the Spanish-speaking people. They had to give them the gospel message.[66] Native Americans and Mexican Americans would soon be "overwhelmed and debauched, and put aside by the incoming of a more stalwart and enterprising race." An effort should be made to reach them with the gospel message, so that "a remnant may be saved" before they disappeared under the advancing Anglo American migration.[67]

Protestant missionaries working among Mexican Americans in the Southwest also saw their work as their part in the realization of the "American Mandate" or "Mission." Protestant America felt a great responsibility in relationship to the rest of the world. The missionaries wanted to convert people to a Protestant understanding of the Christian faith and to disseminate the social, economic, and political values of the United States, which they considered a logical extension of Protestantism. This was particularly important for the people who became U.S. citizens as a result of the Mexican-American War. Protestant ethical, moral, economic, and political values would help them become productive citizens of their new country.

Many considered the United States a land of unique gospel privileges and institutions. They believed that God had prepared the country for a great task. As with Israel in Canaan, God drove out other nations and gave the land to Anglo Americans.[68] But this blessing meant that the United States should be instrumental in "blessing our land and [the] world,"[69] by entering the Southwest with wealth and railroads,[70] for example, and doing away with "the thriftless, unprogressive, and fatalistic mode of life of the native Spanish speaking." Only through evangelization "in the fullest sense of the word" would this new area of the country be established on a "firm and safe political, moral and Christian basis." This task was particularly important among Mexican American U.S. citizens because they were now a part of "our National family."[71] In this effort "patriotism and home missions are inseparably united. Neither can stand, in the mind of the Christian citizen, without the other." New believers were important, but the indirect effects of evangelization "upon the social life, the intellectual spirit, the moral tone, and the public policy, of [all] our western communities are beyond measure."[72]

Toward the end of her life, Emily Harwood lamented the

fact that more had not been done for the "Mexicans" and "native" peoples. She was convinced that the government should have participated in the evangelistic and "enlightenment" process: "There was not the slightest effort made by the government to educate or enlighten them. They were left entirely to the control of the church in matters of education, religion and morals. They must have believed that our nation was a Roman Catholic nation." Her reflections go on to wonder how different things would have been if the government had "entered this field with the schoolmaster, and encouraged the missionary to enter with an open Bible, as has been done in our New Possessions." If the American government had taken the task more seriously, "how different would have been the results of missionary labor" among the Mexicans.[73]

For "Americanization" to be successful, the missionary needed to work in two areas. One was evangelistic. If Christian—that is, Protestant—homes could be developed, where the Bible was read, people prayed and praised God, and the Sabbath was kept, it would be possible to make "the Mexicans good citizens."[74] In his memoirs, Thomas Harwood laments that the "Americanization" process had not been fully successful in New Mexico, because "while the march of civilization had taken grand strides" almost everywhere, a scarcity of Bibles had left that territory behind.[75]

Nonetheless, the Americanization process could not be accomplished merely by evangelizing. Most Protestant missionaries believed that preaching the gospel had to be closely tied to education. For some of the missionary teachers sent to start schools in the small towns of northern New Mexico, education and evangelization were almost synonymous terms. "The work for the evangelization of this people is gaining ground, as may be seen in the good our mission schools are accomplishing."[76] The teachers and those who sent them expected that as children became educated, they would be able to see that they were being enslaved by the priesthood and would throw off that yoke and become "more enlightened and civilized."[77] The missionary schools also aimed to remove the prejudices of the people toward an Anglo American style education. According to Emily Harwood, mission schools were crucial in convincing the people of New Mexico to pass a public school law.[78]

In the eyes of many, these efforts, along with a growing Anglo American population, were preparing the former Mexican territories for statehood. The Christian church and school were working alongside advanced technology, a public school system, and growing American political and commercial control to train "the children of the native population . . . for future citizenship."[79] As statehood became imminent for New Mexico, the mission agencies saw a need to redouble their efforts. Mexican Americans would soon be voters who would influence all of the United States. It was indispensable that Protestants educate and "Americanize" them quickly.[80]

Missionaries also reported successes in "Americanization" of Mexican Americans on an individual level. Thomas Harwood expressed pride in the fact that the few *neomejicanos* who had converted under Methodist missionaries before the Civil War remained loyal to the Union during the war. Three converts joined the Union Army in the Territory.[81] And during the war against Spain (1898), MEC *neomejicanos* again demonstrated strong patriotism. There were "some twenty-five Spanish-speaking ordained Methodist preachers in this mission who would like to go in the U.S. Army as chaplains in the war."[82]

In 1895, the BGC made a detailed analysis of a challenge they attributed to *tejanos* and new immigrants from Mexico and called it one of the most serious problems faced by the Anglo American population of that state. Anglo Americans in Texas, the convention insisted, had to recognize that foreigners entering Texas were there to stay, were gaining control in government, were buying the best agricultural land, and would marry the sons and daughters of the Anglo Americans. Their grandchildren would be of mixed race. "For the sake of the homes and souls of our children and grandchildren," it was crucial that the gospel be preached among these people. It was imperative that the missionaries evangelize immigrants so that Texas would be a good place for their descendants.[83]

Protestant missionaries were particularly concerned about the Territory of New Mexico. Congress had accepted California, Colorado, and Texas as states in the Union because a large number of Anglos had migrated there and the Anglo population was in complete control of the social, economic, and political structures. In New Mexico *neomejicanos* continued in the majority at the end of the nineteenth century. The possibility that New Mexico would gain statehood created concern among the missionaries and provided an important motivation for reaching the *neomejicanos* with the gospel. The "ignorant and bigoted Papists" would soon have a seat in Congress and a place among the sisterhood of states. If a change did not soon occur, New Mexico would enter the Union with all its "illiteracy, ignorance and irreligion."[84]

John Menaul clamored for the Presbyterians of the East Coast to send more missionaries to New Mexico and the West. No American in the East, Menaul insisted, could be indifferent to the situation. The Mexican Americans in the Southwest would influence Anglo Americans migrating west. Sending missionaries to the West was a form of "Gospel Life Insurance." The East was "simply and really providing against a time of need for their children, if not for themselves." The Anglo American Protestant "knows, or should know, that he must either give them his Christianity or they will force their heathenism on him or his posterity."[85]

This fear became greater after Utah became a state in 1896 and Mormons gained a voice in Congress. Protestant leaders felt serious concern about Mexican American Catholics gaining a similar influence. There were 130,000 "bigoted Romanists" in New Mexico, southern Colorado, and Arizona. These people were U.S. citizens, with the right to vote, even though they could not read an English ballot. Because of this, the priests would easily sway them.[86] Toward the end of her life Emily Harwood stated that "the example of Utah since it became a State, is causing us to believe that it is safer for New Mexico to remain a territory for some time yet."[87] Another Presbyterian missionary stated that "this dark plague-spot of moral pollution [New Mexico] must be cleansed, or it will, like its twin sister of Utah, infect the whole body politic."[88]

Americanization stood out as the overarching motive among Protestant missionaries for working with Mexican Americans in the Southwest during the nineteenth century. Missionaries were confident that freeing Mexican Americans from Roman Catholicism would help make them good U.S. citizens, as would a Protestant education and the adoption of North American technology and socioeconomic mores. The Americanization task drew out missionaries and teachers ready to spread the "good news" as they perceived it. Their work was similar, yet different, from that of Protestant missionaries to other countries of the world. Protestant missionaries carried an "Americanized" gospel to other parts of the world. But in the United States, the task of Americanizing converts was overt. For many of the Protestant missionaries, the future of the United States as they knew it depended on the success of their efforts.[89]

4

"Yet Many Do Not Declare Themselves for Fear"

Protestant Mission Efforts Prior to the Civil War

———◆◦◆◦◆———

Brother Nicholson, the Methodist minister . . . gave me this Bible. . . . [I] read the good book. . . . When I woke the sun was shining through the window into my face. The Sun of Righteousness was shining brightly in my soul. I have been a Christian and a Protestant ever since.
Ambrosio Gonzales (1871)

Every day new conversions appear, but as yet many do not declare themselves for fear notwithstanding their conduct makes a favorable impression on the side of Protestantism.
Benigno Cárdenas (1854) quoted in
T. Harwood, *History of New Mexico . . . Missions*

THE ENTHUSIASTIC RHETORIC OF MANY PROTESTANT LEADERS AND mission agencies during and immediately after the war with Mexico did not produce significant missionary efforts among the Mexican Americans in the Southwest. A few tentative efforts were made in Texas and New Mexico, but they all ended by 1861 after a limited response from the Mexican American population, inadequate financial support for the missionaries, and the onset of the Civil War.

Texas

Sumner Bacon, a Cumberland Presbyterian, began working among Anglo American colonists in Mexican *Tejas* in 1829. In 1833 he secured a commission from the American Bible Society to distribute English and Spanish Bibles. He was able to distribute Spanish Bibles among several people, although apparently it violated Mexican law. Bacon found little support for this effort and there were no reported results.

When Texas became an independent republic in 1836, Old School Presbyterians decided to consider it a foreign field. In 1839 the foreign mission board assigned William C. Blair to work among Mexicans in the southwestern part of the republic. Blair arrived in Texas in 1840 and settled in Victoria on the Guadalupe River. He distributed Spanish Bibles and tracts among the Spanish-speaking population. The people graciously received them, even though very few *tejanos* could read. Nonetheless, his principal focus was set on Mexico. Blair was to "avail himself of such opportunities as may offer for sending among them [Mexicans] the knowledge of the truth."[1]

During the early years, Mexican and Indian attacks hampered Blair's efforts. He never recorded any conversions or other results of his efforts, though he reported that, in addition to the Bible and tract distribution, a few Spanish-speaking youth attended his Sunday school classes in Victoria several times before a local priest pressured them to stay away. He always dreamed that Texas would serve as a base for spreading Protestant Christianity into Mexico. After Texas became a state, he started Aranama College where he hoped wealthy Mexican families would send their children. His goal of converting students and returning them home as missionaries was never accomplished, due to financial difficulties and the onset of the Civil War.[2]

The Treaty of Guadalupe Hidalgo (1848) opened the door for Protestant missionaries to work among Mexican Americans in Texas, but only two denominations did so before the Civil War. The first of two Old School Presbyterians, John McCollough, started a Presbyterian church in the San Antonio area. The congregation requested that the city be considered a foreign mission board project, due to its large Spanish-speaking population and close ties with Mexico. McCollough was enthusiastic about the work and reported that several Mexicans were attending the Sabbath school. A Presbyterian mission board sent a converted Spanish priest, Ramón Montsalvage, to work alongside McCollough and start a school for *tejano* children, but local priests reacted so strongly against Montsalvage that he abandoned his efforts. McCollough remained hopeful that his efforts would bear fruit, but ill health forced him to leave San Antonio without seeing any permanent results.[3]

The other Presbyterian missionary in antebellum Texas was Melinda Rankin. She was not commissioned by any mission board, but was able to secure the support of several Presbyterian churches in New England. Rankin arrived in south Texas in 1850 with the purpose of evangelizing Mexicans. Soon after her arrival, she wrote *Texas in 1850* as a challenge to New England Presbyterians to support mission work in Texas and Mexico. In 1852, Rankin decided to settle in Brownsville and continue her efforts from there. In 1854, she secured funds from several Presbyterian churches to begin a school for Spanish-speaking girls. Rankin used the Río Grande Female Institute to make contacts along the border area, distributing Bibles and tracts wherever she could. She was also able to persuade the American Bible So-

ciety to assign Robert Thompson, an MECS minister, as a colporteur to the border area in 1859. He briefly served in the Río
Grande Valley and surrounding areas. Thompson and Rankin
distributed several hundred Spanish Bibles and New Testaments, but there were no reported results of these efforts.

Northern Presbyterians officially accepted the Río Grande
Female Institute as a mission project in 1858 and it remained
open until the start of the Civil War. Soon after the beginning
of the war, Southern Presbyterian leaders forced Rankin to
close the school because it had Northern financial support. The
school reopened after the Civil War, but by then Rankin had entered Mexico and was focusing her ministry energies there. As
with other antebellum Presbyterian efforts, there were no
known conversions.[4]

No MECS missionaries were specifically assigned work
among *tejanos* before the Civil War, but several individuals
learned Spanish and preached in various settings. MECS workers reported their first Mexican American convert at a Methodist camp meeting in Bastrop County, Texas, in 1856. During
that same year, William Headen (called the "Founder of the
Spanish-speaking Work" by H. Horton, an MECS minister of
the period) started a Spanish Sunday school class in Corpus
Christi. Several *tejanos* joined the Methodist Church there, including a man named Antonio Navarro and his daughters.[5] By
1859, the Río Grande Conference of the MECS listed three
Spanish-speaking missions (San Antonio, El Paso, and Laredo)
as places where the conference hoped to appoint workers.[6]
These preliminary efforts were halted due to the Civil War.

Territory of New Mexico

Three Protestant home mission agencies sent workers into the
Territory of New Mexico soon after the United States' takeover
of Santa Fe. The first to send missionaries into this territory was

the American Baptist Convention (Northern) (BAP). Hiram Read and his wife were on their way to California when she took ill in Santa Fe on July 12, 1849. The military commander and governor of the Territory persuaded them to stay, making them the first known Protestant missionaries in New Mexico. Read began a congregation in Santa Fe and decided to learn Spanish. He took on the title of bishop—although Baptists have no bishops—apparently to bolster his influence among the people.[7] Read visited Anglo American and *neomejicano* families and read the Bible to them. He also laid out plans for a school where people could learn to read the Bible.

The American Baptist Missionary Society sent three other missionaries to New Mexico in the 1850s: Lewis Smith, John Shaw, and Samuel Gorman. These workers did not originally plan to work specifically among the Spanish-speaking population, but since there were few Anglo Americans they concentrated their efforts among *neomejicanos* and Native Americans. Smith and Shaw started an English-language congregation in Santa Fe, but chose Albuquerque as the central location for their work among Mexican Americans. In 1853 they organized a church there that included six *neomejicanos:* Blas Chávez, José María Chávez, Reynoldo (Romaldo?) Chávez, J. C. Cohenour, Santos Telles, and Ambrosio Gonzales.[8]

Blas Chávez

From this base the Baptists developed a missionary circuit that eventually included the communities of Isleta, Pajarito, Peralta, Tomé, Los Jarales, and Manzano. The church in Peralta became the largest, reportedly reaching an attendance of 100 people. Baptists also organized an important congregation at

Socorro, which started in 1857 with twenty-two members and at one time reported a congregation of over 100. The communities that had been part of the Albuquerque circuit became a part of a Socorro circuit, and new communities were added, making it the most extensive Baptist preaching circuit in New Mexico. The Baptist missionaries and five *neomejicano* assistants—José María Chávez, Santos Telles, Antonio José García, Blas Chávez, and Romaldo Chávez—served these congregations and preaching points.[9]

The Methodist Episcopal Church (MEC) worked in the same area of central New Mexico as the BAP and established several small congregations, often in the same communities as the Baptists. The MEC sent their first missionary to the Territory of New Mexico a few months after Hiram Read's arrival. Read apparently perceived the Methodist missionary as a threat to Baptist efforts in the Territory.[10] Two events created tensions between the Baptist and Methodist missionaries. The first problem arose over Benigno Cárdenas, a *neomejicano* ex-Roman Catholic priest who became a Methodist minister in New Mexico (more will be said about him in the section on MEC work). Both the Baptists and the Methodists focused their ministry on proving the falseness of Catholic doctrine and considered a person like Cárdenas crucial to their ministry. In 1854 Read contacted Cárdenas and had him preach at several Baptist services. In September of that year Read published a statement claiming that Cárdenas had decided to accept the Baptist rite of baptism by immersion. MEC leaders from the East Coast contacted Cárdenas, who then publicly denied that he had made such a decision and threatened to distance himself from Read and Gorman because of their proselytizing. The Baptist missionaries continued to insist that Cárdenas had made such a commitment before one of the Baptist congregations, but, whether he did or not, he was never baptized as a Baptist.

A second area of contention between Baptists and Methodists

had to do with the work in Peralta. Ambrosio Gonzales is listed as one of the first Baptist converts at Albuquerque. But he was apparently never baptized by immersion.[11] Documents show that Methodist missionaries had also contacted him (it is not clear whether he met the Baptists or the Methodists first) and that he decided to work with them.

As stated earlier, the Baptist missionaries were convinced that they were the best equipped of all Protestant denominations to confront Catholicism. Because of this, Baptists spent much more energy than the Methodists or the Presbyterians on defining themselves over against the other Protestant groups. Mrs. Read once wrote that the people of New Mexico considered Hiram Read to be more correct than the Methodist or Presbyterian missionaries because he was considered a follower of John the Baptist.[12]

Between 1849 to 1860 Baptist missionaries in New Mexico recorded 112 baptisms (not all Mexican Americans). They were able to claim sending the first missionary into the Territory (Hiram Read), organizing the first predominantly Spanish-speaking congregation (Albuquerque), and making the first Mexican American convert (José María Chávez). Nonetheless, the fruit of their labors did not result in a permanent Baptist ministry among *neomejicanos*. All Baptist missionary activity ceased when the Civil War broke out. Read left the territory; Shaw remained, but resigned as a minister and became a shopkeeper in Socorro. When the Methodist missionary Thomas Harwood visited the area in 1873, Shaw encouraged the people he had worked with to join the Methodists, which many did.[13] No other Baptist missionaries worked among *neomejicanos* until the twentieth century.

As mentioned earlier, the MEC sent a missionary into the Territory soon after the Baptists. E. G. Nicholson arrived in New Mexico in 1850 and remained there just one year. He returned to the East, giving a negative report of ministry possibilities in New Mexico. Nonetheless, during his time in New Mexico, Nicholson gave Ambrosio Gonzales a Bible. Gonzales began reading it and accepted the gospel. The first Methodist convert, Gonzales later became a lay leader of the one Methodist congregation that survived after the missionaries left in the mid-1850s.

In 1853 Nicholson returned to the Territory as superintendent of MEC work. He had two assistants, Walter Hansen and the ex-Roman Catholic priest Benigno Cárdenas. Hansen attempted to open a school for Spanish-speaking children in Tecolote in 1854, but it was soon closed due to strong opposition from the Catholic leadership.[14] Soon afterwards Nicholson and Hansen left New Mexico for good and Benigno Cárdenas continued working as a Methodist minister on his own. It was during this time that Read, the Baptist missionary, approached him and encouraged him to join them.

Little is known about Benigno Cárdenas before 1850. He was a priest in *Nuevo Méjico* when it was still a part of Mexico. Cárdenas was one of two priests suspended from the priesthood by the last Mexican bishop over *Nuevo Méjico*, Zubiría of Durango, for reasons not completely understood. He met Nicholson in 1850 and appeared to be attracted to the Methodists. In 1851 Cárdenas apparently traveled to Rome to ask the pope to repeal his suspension. He did not receive the response he desired and, on his way back to New Mexico, spent time with Methodists in London. Upon his return to the United States the Methodists received him and, agreeing to join the MEC mission, he returned to New Mexico with Nicholson and Hansen. The Methodists hoped *neomejicanos* would be attracted to Cárdenas's anti-Catholic preaching. On several occasions Cárdenas challenged Catholic priests to public debates. But Catholic response toward Cárdenas was much more negative than toward other Protestant missionaries. His vitriolic anti-Catholicism was not well received.

After Nicholson and Hansen left, Cárdenas continued an itinerant ministry, preaching his anti-Catholic message in many parts of New Mexico. He apparently was attracted to the Baptists, though it is not clear whether he ever intended to be baptized. He was never ordained as a Methodist minister, although he seems to have baptized infants and performed other rituals usually reserved for ordained clergy. According to Thomas Harwood, most of the work accomplished by the Methodists in the 1850s resulted from Cárdenas' ministry.[15]

When Dalas Lore, an MEC missionary in South America, visited New Mexico in 1855, he found Cárdenas ill. That same year the Methodist home mission board called for workers to join Cárdenas in New Mexico.[16] But Cárdenas never received additional support from the mission board and no other workers ever joined him. When he was close to death, he apparently attempted to reconcile himself with the Catholic Church and possibly received extreme unction on his deathbed.[17]

During his 1855 visit, Lore organized a preaching circuit consisting of four classes: Socorro (nine members), Peralta (fourteen), Jarales (two), and Povadera (four). He arranged the four appointments so that they could be covered in three Sundays.[18] He also organized a class in Belén with two members. Yet Lore's reports were not hopeful enough to encourage the MEC mission board to continue. After Nicholson and Hansen left and Cárdenas died, Methodists did little more in the Territory of New Mexico. No new workers were sent to the Territory before the Civil War, and the work was allowed to "expire."[19]

Nonetheless, the works in Peralta and Socorro survived. When Thomas Harwood visited Peralta in 1871, he found that Ambrosio Gonzales had continued the work assigned to him some sixteen years earlier. The small Bible class had survived and grown to forty-two members. In Socorro, the Baptist church was reorganized as a Methodist congregation under the leadership of several former Baptists, including Blas Chávez and Santos Telles. None of the other early *neomejicano* congregations survived.[20]

The third denomination to work in New Mexico before the

Civil War was the PCUSA (Presbyterian Church in the United States of America [Northern]). They sent Rev. W. J. Kephart to the Territory in 1851. There is no record of any results of his work, and Kephart apparently later became the editor of the *Santa Fe Gazette*.[21]

California

Leonard Pitt, in *Decline of the Californios* (1970), refers to the work of a William Money who started a "Reformed New Testament Church" in Los Angeles in the 1850s. Apparently ten or twelve members of this "offbeat religious sect" were Mexican Americans, including the president and secretary.[22] The movement had no long-term impact in the community.

Mexican American Protestantism before the Civil War

Few mission agencies made serious efforts to work among Mexican Americans in the Southwest before the Civil War, despite the fact that leaders in many Protestant denominations had stated that the conquest of the Southwest would provide an opportunity to convert Mexican Catholics. The few missionaries to Mexican Americans during this period received very little support from their respective mission boards. According to Harwood, Methodist officials concluded that there was no "well grounded hope of establishing an evengelical [*sic*] church in New Mexico" during the 1850s.[23] Apparently this perspective was representative of all Protestant mission agencies.

In the 1850s Protestant missionaries accurately assessed that many Mexican Americans were dissatisfied with the Roman Catholic Church. At the time of the U.S. takeover, there were fewer than twenty active priests among a population of 100,000. The Roman Catholic Church was not able to provide much religious support to the people, and in New Mexico, it had taken actions against the *Penitente* movement. Nonetheless, the missionaries did not understand that dissatisfaction with the Catholic Church would not automatically generate interest in Protestantism and Americanization. By focusing on these themes over against traditional culture, they were able to interest only those who wanted to assimilate into the new culture—a very small percentage of the population during the 1850s.

The rapid increase in westward migration attracted Protestant home mission agencies to the Southwest. But they focused on Anglo and European settlers. Mission agencies ignored the Mexican American population since many Anglo American and European immigrants were settling in places like Northern California, Colorado, and central Texas. The bulk of the Spanish-speaking population lived neither in these areas nor on the routes to them. Therefore, mission agencies, and technological advances, bypassed the Mexican American populations as the new immigrants settled the Southwest.

The growing division between the North and South during the 1850s absorbed much of the energy of Anglo American churches. Most major denominations split over slavery, and their focus in the Southwest centered on "their" people. Work among Mexican Americans was considered a distraction. The Civil War ended all early Protestant missionary efforts among the Spanish speaking, as missionaries returned to their homes or joined the war effort and mission agencies ceased their limited financial support. In one place, Brownsville, Southern leaders closed down the work of a northerner (Melinda Rankin).

Nonetheless, small groups of Latino Protestants developed in Corpus Christi, Texas, and Peralta and Socorro, Territory of New Mexico. When Protestant missionaries returned to the Southwest after the Civil War, these communities were among the first places where Mexican American Protestant churches were organized or reorganized.

5

"Teaching Them to Be Law-abiding, Industrious and Thrifty Citizens"

MEXICAN AMERICAN PROTESTANTISM IN TEXAS

———————

[The new conference was] the key to Mexico's evangelization and the redemption of the whole Southwestern United States.

Texas Christian Advocate (1885)

The terrible night has passed,
Of the world's deception and lying
And the Lord with profound love
Has removed the blindfold from man.

Reynaldo Avila (1904; author's translation)

In giving the Gospel to these people we are not only obeying our risen Lord's command to make disciples of all the nations, but we are rending an inestimable service to our country as well.

Walter Scott (1904)

61

Long-term Protestant mission efforts among Mexican Americans in Texas began after the Civil War. The earliest renewed efforts enjoyed the help of a Mexican convert, Alejo Hernández. While in Mexico, Hernández had found a book, *Evenings with the Romanists*, an anti-Catholic book apparently left in Mexico by one of the soldiers who invaded Mexico during the Mexican-American War. The book left a strong impression on Hernández, and he decided to travel to Brownsville to find a Bible. He attended a small church there and had a conversion experience. He returned to Mexico to share what had happened, but faced such persecution that he decided to return to the United States. In 1870 he joined the Methodist Church in Corpus Christi and was licensed to preach, marking the beginning of a new era of MECS work among Mexican Americans. Hernández preached in various communities and then returned to Mexico with the distinction of being the first licensed Mexican Methodist minister in the Southwest.

Five Protestant denominations worked in Texas in the latter half of the nineteenth century. The MECS reestablished its ministry among *tejanos* as soon as the war ended in 1865. The PCUS and BGC began work toward the end of the 1880s and started experiencing growth as the century came to a close. The MEC and the Disciples of Christ each established one congregation in Texas during the nineteenth century.

Methodist Episcopal Church, South

The MECS came closest to maintaining a ministry among Mexican Americans through the years of the Civil War. Their work among *tejanos* before the Civil War continued until 1862 when several leaders of that effort joined the Confederate Army. Soon after the war ended, they reinitiated the work in Corpus Christi with the help of a Mexican convert, Alejo Hernández.

The Methodists in Corpus Christi officially organized in

1870. In 1872 the West Texas Conference of the MECS assigned
Alexander Sutherland as superintendent of a Spanish-speaking
district within the Conference, and
he went to Corpus Christi to help
strengthen and expand the work
there. A second congregation was
organized in San Diego that same
year. In 1874 three Mexicans from
Monterrey, Mexico, who had been
converted as a result of Melinda
Rankin's work and were recruited
by William Headen (one of the
early leaders in Corpus Christi),
were licensed for ministry among
Mexican Americans by the West
Texas Conference.[1] From this point

Alejo Hernández

the Methodist work began to grow. The preachers, all being circuit riders, did not limit themselves to their official appointments.[2] By 1877 there were ten established congregations in
Texas with 432 members.

During these early years, the work expanded from Corpus
Christi toward central and west Texas and down to several border towns on the Río Grande (Map 1). The West Texas Conference also established congregations on the Mexican side of the
border. By 1880 MECS efforts had advanced to such a point
that a second Spanish-speaking district was organized in the
West Texas Conference. That year the district reported sixteen
churches with 709 adult members. In 1883 the West Texas
Conference approved a resolution calling for the formation of a
school, the Anglo-Mexico College, to train Spanish-speaking
workers for Texas and Mexico.[3] The number of reported congregations decreased to fourteen in 1884, with little membership growth until that year. In 1885 fifteen churches and a slight
increase in membership were reported.[4]

An important factor in Methodist growth during these early years was the number of Mexican American pastors. Alexander Sutherland recruited many who took leadership in extending Methodism into new communities. They were recent converts who had a great deal of enthusiasm and commitment to the task. By the mid-1870s almost all of the MECS' Spanish-language churches in Texas were being pastored by Mexican Americans.

As early as 1877, the West Texas Conference resolved to ask the General Conference to approve the formation of the Mexican Border Mission District into a separate annual conference.[5] The General Conference took no action on the request until 1884, when it approved the formation of the Mexican Border Mission Conference, which joined MECS work in Texas with ministry in northern Mexico. This new mission conference came under the foreign mission board. The board organized the Mexican Border Mission Conference into four presiding elder districts, two based in Texas (San Antonio and El Paso) and two in Mexico (Monterrey and Monclova). This decision was greatly praised by the superintendent of the new conference, Alexander Sutherland, as a first in Mexican missions and a great opportunity to expand the work in Mexico and among Spanish-speaking communities in the United States.[6] The editor of the *Texas Christian Advocate* described the new conference as the one that covered the most territory and worked among the most needy population, and with it, Methodists held "the key to Mexico's evangelization and the redemption of the whole Southwestern United States."[7]

However, this new organizational structure created difficulties for MECS work in Texas and adversely affected mission efforts there. For one thing, it raised the question of the propriety of work in Texas being supported by the foreign mission board, since this created an anomalous situation in which work among *tejanos* officially became a foreign mission effort.[8] It reinforced the notion common among Southern Methodists that

Spanish-language churches in Texas were foreign. Moreover, the Mexican Border Mission Conference focused most of its efforts on Mexico, which adversely affected ministry in Texas. The years from 1885 to 1900 experienced a net gain of only two churches in Texas, while during that same period, the number of churches on the Mexican side of the conference increased from nineteen to thirty.[9]

In 1891 the Border Mission Conference was divided in two: churches in central and south Texas remained in the Mexican Border Mission Conference and those in west Texas became a part of the new Northwest Mexican Conference. This decision split Mexican American Methodists in Texas, as their churches in various parts of the state no longer had any formal connections. The formation of the Northwest Mexican Conference in 1891 responded to ministry needs in Mexico, not Texas. None-

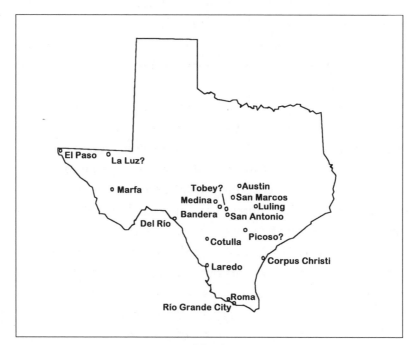

Map 1
Mexican American Methodist Episcopal Church, South Churches, 1900
Texas

theless, though few new churches were started, existing *tejano* churches continued to grow, and by 1900 seventeen Spanish language congregations reported 1450 adult members.

The affiliation of *tejano* Methodist churches with Mexico continued into the twentieth century. This relationship did not change until 1914, when the Mexican Revolution made ministry in Mexico difficult and forced many Mexicans to migrate to the United States. Only then did MECS ministries among the Mexican Americans of Texas return to home mission jurisdiction as the Mexican Mission of Texas.

Presbyterian Church in the United States

To encourage work among *tejanos* before the Civil War, some Presbyterians had argued that Texas was a "great doorway to Mexico."[10] But this argument lost its force when missionaries were allowed to enter Mexico after the Civil War. The PCUS therefore sent missionaries to Mexico before sending anyone to work among *tejanos*. PCUS ministry in Texas began as a result of work done in Mexico.

Not only did PCUS ministry originate in Mexico rather than in the U.S., it was also begun by a local congregation rather than by a mission board. A Presbyterian congregation in the Mexican border town of Matamoros, Tamaulipas, sent workers to its sister town, Brownsville, on the American side of the Río Grande. The church was not large, but its leaders sent missionaries to the Mexicans in Texas. A church was organized in Brownsville in 1877, becoming the first PCUS congregation among *tejanos*. Because of its ties to Matamoros, this congregation remained a part of the Mexican Presbytery of Tamaulipas well into the twentieth century. It was never a part of the West Texas Presbytery and was not included when the Mexican American congregations of Texas organized themselves into a presbytery in the first part of the twentieth century.[11]

The Matamoros Presbyterian Church also played a crucial role in the nascent PCUS work among *tejanos* in central Texas. José María Botello,[12] an elder in the Matamoros congregation (and possibly a worker in Brownsville), moved to San Marcos in 1885 to begin evangelistic work among *tejanos*. By the time he returned to Matamoros in 1886, ten Mexican Americans had joined the Presbyterian Church of San Marcos. In 1887 the group had grown to 26 adults and numerous children. That year the congregation petitioned for admission into the West Texas Presbytery as a church. The group's leaders were examined, and the San Marcos congregation was accepted into the Presbytery in November of that year.

José María Botello

A key person at the examination meeting was Walter Scott, who was born in Mexico to Scottish Calvinist and French Huguenot parents and whose family moved to Texas when he was thirteen. Melinda Rankin was working in Monterrey when Scott was a small boy and had an influence on him. Scott's bilingual abilities and interest in missionary work led him to help MECS efforts among *tejanos* in San Antonio. In 1885—the same year that Botello moved to San Marcos—Scott contacted the PCUS group in San Marcos and began working with them. When the church was organized in 1887, he served as translator. The West Texas Presbytery accepted him as a candidate for gospel ministry, and he continued to work with the San Marcos congregation while he studied at Austin Presbyterian Seminary. In 1892 the West Texas Presbytery ordained Scott for ministry among *tejanos* (even though he never finished seminary) marking a new era in PCUS evangelism among Mexican Americans.

Walter Scott and Mexican PCUS pastors and leaders. Seated, left to right: Salinas, Scott, Cárdenas; standing, left to right: García, Alba, Samaniego, Pérez. Picture first appeared in The Texas Presbyterian, March 5, 1896.

From 1887 to 1892 the San Marcos congregation, with sixty-seven members, was the only existing Spanish-language PCUS church in central Texas. After Scott's ordination to ministry, new churches were organized in Martindale and Uvalde in 1893. Scott was the official pastor of all three congregations because he was the only ordained pastor, and all organized PCUS churches had to have an ordained minister as titular pastor. Nonetheless, Scott had valuable assistance: Juan Hernández, originally licensed to work with the San Marcos congregation, served in Uvalde, and Julio Avila was licensed to serve in Martindale.[13] In 1896 new congregations were also organized in Corpus Christi and Laredo. The Presbytery assigned Hernández to Laredo, and Scott continued as the principal worker in the Central Texas congregations. Henry Pratt, former missionary to Colombia, joined the work in Laredo in 1896.[14] Under these leaders, new congregations were established in Reedville

(1897), Beeville (1900), and Victoria (1900) (Map 2). Pratt also organized a Bible institute in Laredo. The program of study focused on biblical memorization and interpretation and purposely did not provide a broad education so that the pastors would not be tempted to seek other employment or leave their poor communities.[15] The first three graduates, Reynaldo Avila, Abram Fernández, and Elías Treviño, were licensed in 1900.

In 1900 there were eight organized *tejano* PCUS churches with 517 members.[16] By 1903 there were 13 organized congregations with 680 members, 21 elders, 17 deacons, 2 evangelists, 3 ordained *tejano* pastors, and 7 church buildings.[17] In 1908, 17 *tejano* congregations organized themselves into the Texas-Mexican Presbytery.

According to Scott, these early efforts produced converts who did not easily turn back from their new faith, and he was very proud of the "trophies of our work."[18] Yet the congregations did not have a strong membership or financial base. Most of the Mexican American Presbyterian churches were small and

Henry Pratt, seated, with the first graduates of his Bible institute in 1898. Left to right, Reynaldo Avila, Elías Treviño, and Abraham Fernández.

dependent on the presbytery for financial support. The few committed converts could not take leadership and financial responsibility for their congregations. Scott stated that this was because of "the besotted ignorance and gross superstitiousness of the people, and the men and means at our command, as in the regular work of the Church among Americans."[19] In spite of the limited progress during the nineteenth century, Scott defended the work being done by stating that it was cheaper to produce a Mexican convert than an American one[20] and that there was a good foundation in the character of the people to "build up, with the blessing of God, a strong, self-propagating and self-sustaining church in the future."[21]

Baptist General Convention

The third group to engage in ministry among *tejanos* during the nineteenth century was the Baptist General Convention of Texas (Southern Baptist). They began talking about work among *tejanos* as early as 1858.[22] The Blanco Baptist Association in south central Texas began mentioning the need to work among the "Mexican" population in 1879.[23] For the next two decades most of the annual conventions of the association included reports "On Mexican and Colored Population," which varied from very enthusiastic and optimistic to almost hopeless. An 1880 report mentioned the work of Methodists and stated that "some of these Mexicans are Baptist in principle, and would unite with us if an opportunity were offered."[24] An 1881 report praised the efforts of T. M. Westrup (one of the first Southern Baptist missionaries in Mexico) and expressed that "the prospects for missionary efforts among the Mexicans are very encouraging . . . we should supply them with a missionary as soon as possible to supply the great destitution among them."[25] The 1882 report was neither as optimistic nor as knowledgeable about the work among Mexican Americans. Yet the document challenged the association and the denomination at large to work among the Mexican population, because "from the best information at our command we believe that evangelical christianity [*sic*] is fast taking hold of the Mexican mind." The committee suggested that the association establish a Mexican mission in Corpus Christi, "as soon as practicable."[26]

The 1884 report expressed much less possibility. The author recognized that his knowledge was limited, since he was not the chairperson, but he found it difficult to report favorably. Mexicans "seem rather to be retrograding than advancing," possibly due "to the influence of other religions of less spiritual power." The report states that it was important to work among the Mexicans, but lamented that "there is nothing to be done by us for the Mexicans, because we have no minister who can speak the language."[27] The 1885 report included a long lament over the state of Mexicans in Texas. The author's "heart grows sick with sadness over the awful condition of the Mexican" because he was alone and there was "no eye to pity him, no God to save." The average American showed no pity toward the Mexican because "his former deeds of treachery have closed the doors of charity against him."[28] According to the report, there were a few Mexican Methodists and only three Baptist converts in Texas. The author hoped that God "in His own good time" would "devise some means by which these perishing thousands shall be brought to Christ."[29]

The Blanco Association's reports of the "Mexican and Colored Population Committee" throughout the 1880s and 1890s continued to speak of the need to reach *tejanos*, vacillating between encouragement and pessimism. All this early rhetoric did not immediately translate into concrete action. The BGC established churches in Mexico before it did among the Spanish-speaking communities in Texas; Southern Baptists seemed much more interested in sending missionaries to Mexico than to *tejanos*.[30]

Baptists nevertheless made their first contacts with *tejanos* around 1880. Thomas Westrup and William Flournoy were assigned to work in Mexico, but apparently Flournoy spent some time on the Texas side of the border. According to BGC tradition, Flournoy organized a Spanish-speaking church in Laredo in 1883,[31] which was later abandoned and apparently had no lasting results. The first Spanish-speaking congregation officially reported by the BGC General Convention was organized in San Antonio in 1887.[32] William Powell, a missionary to Mexico, had returned to the States due to an illness in the family. While in Texas, he began working in a Spanish-speaking community in San Antonio. A congregation was organized with nine members, and Manuel Treviño, an MECS minister who had been expelled from the Mexican Border Mission Conference,[33] became the pastor of the new church (upon Powell's recommendation).[34] That same year the BGC State Board assigned Treviño and Mina Everett, who had intended to go to Mexico, as missionaries to the Mexicans of Texas.

In 1889 Treviño reported a congregation of twenty-five in San Antonio. He also helped organize another church in San Marcos with twenty-six members.[35] The 1890 report of the San Antonio Baptist Association mentioned a new project at Pecos, naming Pio Qunto Ybaben [*sic*] as pastor. Other parts of the "Mexican" report stated that there were 5 missionaries employed, 82 baptisms, 86 new members received by the mission churches, 4 received by letter, and 1 church organized. Nonetheless, the statistical table of the association for 1890 only reports membership for San Antonio.[36]

In 1891 the Texas State Board of the BGC assigned C. D. Daniel, as "general missionary to the Mexicans," a decision greatly praised at the time as an opportunity to expand BGC work in this area.[37] The appointment liberated Treviño to work as an evangelist. He started a congregation in New Berlin and reported another, although statistical reports do not include it.

Everything pointed to favorable results. "The record of the year emphasized our belief that the Mexicans in Texas can be reached easily and cheaply."[38]

Statistical reports for 1891 list five missionaries to the Mexicans of Texas (Everett, M. G. Treviño, A. P. Treviño, Daniel, and Ybaben) and state that Daniel and Ybaben each organized two churches and that Treviño organized one.[39] However, the General Convention statistical report for 1891 does not include membership totals, and the San Antonio Association only lists membership for the congregations in San Antonio, San Marcos, and New Berlin.[40]

In 1892, BGC work expanded into El Paso. According to Baptist reports, Alex Marchand, a French ex-priest and pastor of a Methodist church in the city, became convinced of the validity of Baptist doctrine—likely a reference to believers' baptism by immersion—and persuaded several members of the church to help him organize a Spanish-speaking Baptist church.[41] It grew quickly and by 1893 had 100 members.[42] The 1892 report also mentions a new congregation in Reedville with twenty-seven members. By this time the minutes of the San Antonio Baptist Association listed four Spanish-speaking congregations.[43] The 1892 General Convention report was very encouraging, mentioning a new congregation at San Angelo, generally lauding the work being done among Mexican Americans.[44]

The 1893 reports reflect internal problems. Treviño and another pastor, R. E. del Valle, unexpectedly resigned (Treviño later continued working with the Baptists), and work came to a standstill in San Marcos, Reedville, and Martindale. Apparently there were tensions between Treviño and Daniel.[45] Conference reports did not directly mention the problems, but described the work among Mexican Americans as "unsatisfactory."[46]

It is difficult to reconstruct the status of Baptist work in 1893. The General Convention minutes give two versions of the number of Spanish-speaking BGC churches. In one place the report states that "there are now nine churches, two more than were reported last year. San Antonio, San Marcos, Reedville, Del Rio, New Berlin, Pecos, Laredo, San Angelo and El Paso."[47] In another place the minutes say that "we have 200,000 Mexicans with only seven churches, scattered from El Paso to Laredo."[48] Statistical reports do not mention membership totals for any of these congregations. The statistical table for the San Antonio Association gives two different membership totals for San Marcos: 58 and 105.[49] The Blanco Baptist Association minutes for 1893 do not mention a congregation at Laredo. The only solid data available for 1893 is from the San Antonio Baptist Association and a report written by the Baptist historian B. F. Fuller in 1900.[50]

The reports for 1894 are even more confusing. The BGC report speaks highly of the work of Manuel Treviño in the San Antonio and Río Grande associations. It states that two Mexican missionaries were appointed by the latter association and praises the work being done by Alex Marchand, who was working around El Paso, in both Mexico and New Mexico, and who needed several assistants. The State Convention statistical table states that Manuel Treviño organized one church but does not specify which one. The San Antonio Association report mentions a new congregation at Calaveras, but only listed membership totals for that congregation.[51]

From 1895 to 1900 statistical reports are incomplete. The statistical table of the San Antonio Association does not list any Spanish-speaking congregations, even though most *tejano* Baptist churches belonged to that association. Río Grande Association minutes mention that it had one Mexican missionary, but do not include statistical reports for any churches. The state convention report refers to Manuel García in the Río Grande Association and Marchand in El Paso. But according to the report on the "Mexican" work, "like the work among the Germans, that among the Mexicans moves slowly. The yoke of Rome with ignorance and superstition makes it very difficult to reach these people."[52] The enthusiasm of the early years had been lost. There would be no more reporting in association minutes of BGC work among Mexican Americans until the twentieth century. The lack of solid statistical data in conference reports also suggests that the reported Spanish-speaking congregations were not yet clearly established, and that conference statisticians were not always fully aware of their status.

The few extant records of BGC work during the nineteenth century seem to suggest that it did grow, but slowly. In his 1931 Ph.D. dissertation, William Miller, using the BGC missionary C. D. Daniel as his source, reports that there were five Mexican Baptist preachers in 1896 and about 200 members. He also reports that the church in El Paso dwindled to only a dozen members then fell apart.[53] According to the historian Fuller, there were

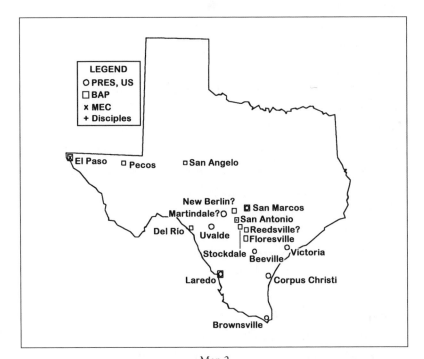

Map 2
Mexican American Baptist General Convention, Methodist Episcopal Church,
Presbyterian Church, US, and Disciples of Christ Churches, 1900
Texas

nine "Mexican" Baptist churches in Texas in 1900.[54] But his list does not include Stockdale, which was started in 1896 (according to Miller[55]) and is listed in 1901 statistical reports. All of this seems to confirm Miller's assessment that Baptists carried on their work among *tejanos* with "indifferent zeal" until 1906.[56]

Methodist Episcopal Church

The New Mexico Spanish Mission Conference of the MEC began work in El Paso in 1886 (although it reported no membership until 1888). It reported solid growth from 1888 to 1891 and maintained a somewhat stable membership from 1892 to 1894. It then reported a heavy loss in 1895. Extant records do not explain the reason for this sudden drop, and by 1900 it had partially recovered from the loss.[57]

During the 1890s, the New Mexico Conference also began working in Juárez, Chihuahua (Mexico), though no membership was reported for the work in Mexico during the nineteenth century. But these efforts did not produce a major expansion of the New Mexico Spanish Mission Conference into Texas or northern Chihuahua. Alex Marchand, who later became a Baptist, pastored the El Paso MEC congregation from 1887 to 1892. MEC records report a membership loss of sixteen members in 1892 when Marchand became a Baptist and reportedly took Methodist church members with him to form the Mexican Baptist Church (BGC) of El Paso. It is unclear whether the membership loss reported in 1895 was related to this issue.[58]

Disciples of Christ

A Disciples of Christ publication mentions a mission among the Spanish speaking in San Antonio in 1888. But there is no other nineteenth-century reference to this project. A later survey of Disciples of Christ work states that in 1899 "a number of persons" were baptized and a Mexican church was organized in San Antonio under the leadership of Y. Quintero. Little is known about the congregation until 1908 when it was reorganized with fourteen members under the leadership of a missionary that came from Mexico.[59]

Mexican American Protestants in Texas, 1900

In 1900 Protestant denominations reported 2,378 Mexican American adult Protestant church members in Texas (Graph 1). Almost two-thirds belonged to the Methodist Episcopal Church, South. The other third belonged to the Presbyterian Church, US, Baptist General Convention, Methodist Episcopal Church, and the Disciples of Christ. Most of the churches were located in central Texas, with a few MECS and Baptist churches in west Texas (Maps 1 and 2). Only the MECS had churches

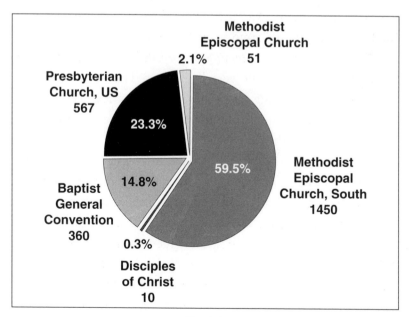

Graph 1
Mexican American Protestants, 1900
Texas

south of Laredo in the Río Grande Valley.[60]

As noted in Chapter 3, Protestant missionary work among *tejanos* was tied to Mexico from the very beginning. In practical terms this meant that new Protestant growth among *tejanos* during the nineteenth century was closely linked to churches already begun in Mexico. Each denomination drew many of their key early leaders for their work among *tejanos* from congregations recently established south of the border. For instance, people who came from Mexico started the first Spanish-language PCUS church in Brownsville and the first BGC church in San Antonio. This was also the case with the PCUS Church in San Marcos. Alejo Hernández, who served as a catalyst for a renewed MECS commitment in 1870, had then recently arrived from Mexico. The first three Mexican American MECS pastors in Texas, Doroteo García, José María Casanova, and Clemente Vivero, were recruited from MECS work in Mexico, and throughout the nineteenth century MECS pastors in Texas often came from there. Walter Scott (PCUS) and Manuel Treviño (BGC) also originally came from Mexico.

This situation gave *tejano* Protestantism a Mexican and "foreign" flavor from the very beginning. The MECS affirmed this foreignness by tying *tejano* churches to conferences in Mexico. But other denominations also treated *tejano* Protestants as foreigners, even if they were part of U.S. church structures. *Tejano* Protestants were treated as Mexicans and they developed an identity closely linked to Mexican Protestantism until well into the twentieth century. Though one of the stated goals of the Protestant missionaries was to teach *tejanos* to be good American citizens, their efforts did not include treating the converts as "true" Americans. *Tejano* Protestants clearly had a second-class status in Protestant church structures. Protestant missionaries had a sense of racial superiority that convinced them that *tejanos* could never be "real" Protestants, but they also reflected a fear of a *tejano* takeover of Protestant church structures. Living in the Borderlands meant that *tejano* Protestants would be treated as foreigners, even by their co-religionists.

Yet this situation also provided *tejano* Protestants a small space in which to develop their own leaders and church structures. These congregations served as a support system for the converts, but also as a place to begin defining what it meant to be "Mexican," Protestant, and a citizen of the United States.

6

"A Slumbering People"

MEXICAN AMERICAN PROTESTANTISM
IN THE TERRITORY OF NEW MEXICO

———◆◆◆◆———

While the march of civilization had taken grand strides almost everywhere else, New Mexico had fallen behind. Why? For want of Bibles, schools and proper instruction.
Thomas Harwood (1870)

[W]hen the boys and girls can read good English literature, their minds may be molded in the right way.
The Home Missionary (1888)

[Work among the Spanish-speaking people of the United States] is too foreign to enlist the sympathy, so freely given by a large class of our church, to work among neglected or needy English speaking people in our cities and on our frontier. . . . Observation leads me to believe that this disadvantage lies more heavily upon the work among the Spanish-speaking citizens of New Mexico.
David H. Moore (1903)

IN 1869 THE PCUSA WOMEN'S MISSIONARY SOCIETY COMMISsioned John A. Annin as a missionary to work among the Spanish speaking of New Mexico. The Women's Missionary Society did not have the full blessing of the PCUSA home mission board when they commissioned Annin. Board secretary H. Kendall felt that Annin should focus on the English-speaking population and that Spanish-speaking communities should not be a "first priority."[1]

Kendall's attitude typifies the priorities of the denominations that worked in this territory. When Protestant missionaries returned to New Mexico after the Civil War, their principal focus continued being English-speaking U.S. citizens. But because *neomejicanos* comprised such an overwhelming majority of the population, the PCUSA and the MEC went on to devote significant energy to establishing churches among them. A third denomination, the Congregationalists, developed a small ministry that had a minimal impact.

Presbyterian Church in the United States of America

John Annin arrived in Las Vegas, New Mexico, in October 1869 to begin the first Presbyterian work among *neomejicanos*. Despite the lack of full support by the PCUSA home mission board, the Women's Missionary Society went forward with their plans and became the principal funding agency for PCUSA work among Mexican Americans during the nineteenth century.

Annin found that there was one *neomejicano* Protestant in the Las Vegas area, José Inés (also Ynés) Perea. Perea had been sent by his parents to study in St. Louis and while there had become a Protestant. Perea's new faith estranged him from his family when he returned to New Mexico, but he continued to live near them in Las Vegas. Perea considered Annin's arrival an answer to prayer and he committed to supporting Annin's ministry efforts. Annin organized a Presbyterian church in Las Vegas in 1870 with eight charter members, including five *neomejicanos*. Perea became the congregation's first elder. Annin began training Perea and Rafael Gallegos, an early convert, for ministry. Together they visited neighboring communities and ranches, preaching and distributing tracts and Bibles. The Las Vegas church received the few converts until PCUSA churches were established in Ocaté (1875) and Agua Negra (1881).

A second base for work among *neomejicanos* was started in Taos by James Roberts, who arrived there in 1872 with the goal of working among the Navajo. But due to strong opposition from the native population, he learned Spanish and began a school as a means of gaining an entrance among the people.[2] By 1874 he had organized a predominantly Spanish-speaking PCUSA congregation in Taos. Roberts also organized a group of *neomejicano* men and began to train them for ministry. Among these men were Vicente Romero and Pablo Ortega, who would later serve as evangelists in several communities.

Roberts and his group began visiting several communities. In Ocaté they found a former *Penitente*, Amadeo Maés, who, with the help of friends and at great cost, had obtained a Bible (the Ocaté Bible, of which more will be said later). Maés and his friends and neighbors had been gathering secretly to study the Bible. When Roberts arrived, he found a group of about twenty people, whom he organized into a congregation in 1875.

Presbyterians and Penitentes

During the Spanish and Mexican rule in New Mexico a lay religious order called the Cofradía de Cristo Jesús Nazareno (Penitentes) thrived in the northern part of the Territory. Because there were few priests, particularly in northern New Mexico and southern Colorado, the people developed their own religious support system. This lay order functioned as a mutual aid society and provided the religious services that could be performed by lay people. The Penitentes were strongest in the areas of northern New Mexico, particularly near Taos, that were the most isolated and least frequented by priests.[3]

The Catholic hierarchy did not condone the order because its members also practiced various forms of physical penitence. However, several local priests supported the *Penitentes*, including Father Antonio José Martínez, a leader among *neomejicano* priests during the 1840s and 1850s. When the United States took over the Southwest, the American Catholic Church assumed responsibility of the Catholic churches in the region. The U.S. Catholics had a very negative view of Mexican Catholicism and assigned a French priest, Jean Baptiste Lamy, as bishop of Santa Fe. Lamy was determined to straighten things out and took actions against several priests, including Martínez, and also attempted to control the *Penitentes*. Martínez was suspended in 1858, but continued performing religious ceremonies and providing religious and moral support to several *Penitente* fraternities until his death in 1867.

Many local *cofradías* (local groups of *Penitentes*) in northern New Mexico became disenchanted with Lamy and the Catholic Church hierarchy. When James Roberts arrived in the area he attracted several *Penitentes* who hoped to find religious freedom and support. Two of the first converts, José Mondragón and Vicente Romero,[4] had been followers of Martínez and *Penitentes*. Later, several Presbyterian congregations in northern New Mexico and southern Colorado developed around a nucleus of former *Penitentes*.

Education as Mission

The PCUSA was convinced that education was crucial to their missionary mandate. The Women's Missionary Society, which made the original commitment to support the work among Mexican Americans in New Mexico, strongly supported educational efforts as part of their mission mandate. With their support, missionary teachers established "plaza" schools—so called because they were started wherever there was a plaza, a small community—in approximately fifty communities. The goal was for these schools to remain open until a public school was started in each community. By 1879 there were three predominantly *neomejicano* congregations and eleven schools "among the Mexicans."[5] This trend continued throughout the nineteenth century and into the twentieth, until the United States government established public schools in most communities.

Sending as many or more missionary teachers as church-planting missionaries to New Mexico formed part of the Presbyterian view of missions. *Neomejicanos* were considered a "foreign" mission field and Presbyterian mission strategy at the time often focused on education when it entered a new area. According to Sheldon Jackson (1874) Presbyterians needed to approach New Mexico the same way they approached Persia or India, where establishing schools played an integral part in their mission strategy.[6]

Teachers were the first "missionaries" to many communities that later had Spanish-speaking churches. PCUSA teachers, mostly single females, were considered missionaries who could go where a regular missionary could not venture. They offered something community people wanted: education for their children. And because they were women, Catholic males did not directly attack them. The people might not yet be ready to openly accept Protestantism, but they would see that Protestant schools were superior and would eventually accept the faith upon which they were based.[7]

The Women's Society funded the teachers and provided the money to build schools; over $100,000 was spent on buildings alone during the nineteenth century. These buildings served as school buildings, chapels, and even as homes for the teachers and missionaries. By 1900 over forty-six schools had functioned or were functioning, more than the number of churches planted. Many of these schools were short-lived, but as the twentieth century began there were twenty-four active schools in the Territory of New Mexico, four in Colorado, and one in California. These were staffed by fifty-two teachers and had almost 2,000 students.[8]

Leadership Development

Presbyterians in New Mexico and Colorado maintained very high educational requirements for ordination. While the MEC and MECS lowered their requirements so that they could ordain Mexican American leaders, the PCUSA did not.[9] And all organized churches were required to have an ordained pastor. Therefore, denominational reports usually listed *neomejicano* leaders as "helpers" or "evangelists." Ordained Anglo missionaries served as the titular pastors of most Mexican American Presbyterian churches.

The various areas where there were PCUSA missions and schools were divided into "fields." Each of these had an ordained pastor who oversaw the schools and congregations in his area. He took the various "native" evangelists under his wing and trained them for ministry. These "lay ministers" or "evangelists" did much of the actual work of reaching out to their own people, making contacts in new and often isolated communities, leading the congregations between visits from the ordained pastor, and directly facing the tensions and opposition in the communities where they served. The PCUSA licensed the first *neomejicano* evangelists in 1877. In 1880 José Inés Perea became the first ordained *neomejicano* PCUSA pastor. He qualified earlier than the other Mexican American leaders because he had studied in American schools during his youth.

In 1890 one of the newer missionaries, James Gilchrist,[10] and his brother, Francis, organized a summer institute for the evangelists. Students worked as paid evangelists three days per week and studied the other four. The institutes lasted from twelve to fourteen weeks and included subjects such as Bible, theology, homiletics, church history, and also geography and arithmetic.[11] In the 1890s *neomejicanos* were also sent to the Presbyterian College of the Southwest in Del Norte, Colorado, for pastoral training.[12]

Overview of PCUSA Work in the Territory of New Mexico

The first predominantly Spanish-speaking PCUSA church was organized in Las Vegas in 1870. It experienced little growth during its first years of existence. The second congregation, established in Taos in 1874, also remained small during its first years. Ten years later (1880) there were four congregations with a total of 132 members: Las Vegas, Taos, Ocaté, and Agua Negra (Holman). Agua Negra first had a mission school led by one of the *neomejicano* evangelists, Rafael Gallegos. John Eastman then organized a church there.

Presbyterians began sending new missionaries and school teachers into New Mexico in the early 1880s. Some were assigned to communities already set as PCUSA preaching points. Others established themselves in new communities, mostly in northern New Mexico. A few were assigned to new areas in central and southern New Mexico. The results of their work became evident in the late 1880s and early 1890s when several new churches were officially organized.

John Annin and his team of *neomejicano* evangelists preached in various small communities. In 1879 he organized a congregation in El Rito (Chacón), although it was not officially listed in conference statistics until 1883. The core of this congregation consisted of several Protestant *neomejicano* families from the nearby community of Chamisal who had left their homes and moved to Chacón, due to persecution by Catholic neighbors.[13] In 1881 the PCUSA mission board assigned another missionary, Maxwell Phillips, to work in Mora. He was to organize a church and a school and serve as overseer for existing schools in the area.

With the help of J. D. Mondragón, one of the evangelists from Taos, a congregation was organized in Mora in 1882. James Roberts also organized a congregation for the cluster of villages around Rincones, Peñasco, and El Valle in 1881. Another church was established at Pajarito in 1884. Churches were also established—and closed—in Rancho de Taos, Mesilla, and Peralta.

The first fifteen years of a Presbyterian presence in New Mexico resulted in nine organized churches with a total of 279 members (see Statistical Table in Appendix). Most were located in the northern part of the Territory of New Mexico (Costilla, Taos, El Rito/Chacón, Rincones, Ocaté, Agua Negra, Mora, and Las Vegas), and there was also a congregation (Pajarito) in the central part of New Mexico (see Map 4).

Presbyterian work among *neomejicanos* grew the most between 1885 and 1895. The number of churches grew as missionaries, local evangelists, and converts began new congregations throughout the Sangre de Cristos Mountains. From 1885 to 1895 twenty-two *neomejicano* congregations were officially organized and reported members at least one year. Of these, eighteen were still in existence in 1895. It is not always easy to determine when some of the congregations were started, because the missionaries often organized congregations years before they were ever listed as churches in official statistical reports. All these churches were officially organized and pastored by the missionaries (except Los Lentes, which was organized by Perea) because only ordained PCUSA pastors could fulfill these functions.[14]

Growth slowed after 1895. Only one new congregation was organized from 1896–1900 (Jarales 1896). During this period the churches experienced a net growth of twenty-three members, bringing the total to 908 in 1900.[15]

None of the *neomejicano* congregations was ever large. In 1900 only five of the twenty-nine churches reported over fifty members, and only El Rito had over one hundred members (127). The average size of a congregation was thirty-one mem-

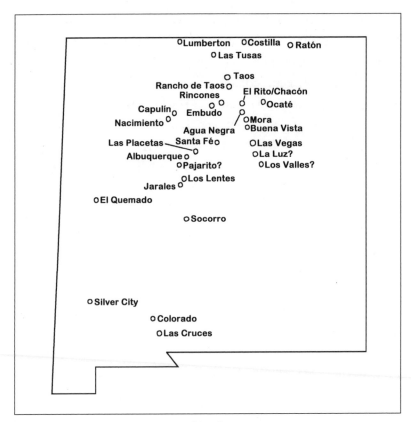

Map 3
Mexican American Presbyterian Church, USA Churches, 1900
Territory of New Mexico

bers, fewer than in 1885, when the membership average was thirty-five. This was due, in large part, to the fact that most of the churches were located in very small communities.[16]

The PCUSA was able to establish itself and grow in New Mexico because it focused on meeting felt needs of some of the population: education for the children and an alternative to Roman Catholicism. It performed services that, at the time, were not being provided by the U.S. government or the Catholic Church. Because it sent many single women as teachers, it was able to enter areas where male Protestant missionaries would not have been welcome. These educational efforts did not always produce churches, but they did open many communities to the Protestant witness. PCUSA commitment to education also created a long-term relationship between the denomination and the communities where Presbyterian teachers worked. When the advancing Anglo American "civilization" completely bypassed these communities, Presbyterians remained in them and provided schools, clinics, and small churches.

Presbyterians also capitalized on *Penitente* disenchantment with the U.S. Catholic hierarchy. Their openness toward the *Penitentes* provided ministry opportunities that they might not have had otherwise, producing direct results in several isolated communities of northern New Mexico and southern Colorado, where the lay order was the strongest. Many former *Penitente* leaders found spaces as leaders of the new *neomejicano* Presbyterian churches.

Despite these achievements, Presbyterian efforts never produced the number of converts they expected. Successful schools did not convince many *neomejicanos* to become Presbyterians. Presbyterian polity concerning ordination also limited the development of *neomejicano* leaders. Many of the successful church leaders did not qualify for ordination because of their limited schooling.

The PCUSA also faced the problem of economic viability. The schools and churches were dependent on outside financial support. Home mission agencies provided the funds for buildings and salaries. They did not develop structures that could be supported by the *neomejicano* communities. In short, Presbyterian work among the Spanish speaking in the Territory could exist only as long as it was being funded from the outside.

Methodist Episcopal Church

MEC work among Mexican Americans in nineteenth-century New Mexico is largely the story of Thomas and Emily Harwood. The couple went to the Territory in 1869 and lived in New Mexico for forty years. They largely defined the focus and direction of the work during the nineteenth century and into the first part of the twentieth. When the Harwoods first arrived in La Junta, New Mexico, in 1869, they intended to work among the English-speaking population. But they found work in the Spanish-speaking community "far more encouraging" and decided to concentrate their efforts among the *neomejicano* population.[17]

The Harwoods formed part of the Methodist Episcopal Church (MEC) resumption of missionary work in New Mexico four years after the end of the Civil War. Some of the leaders from the earlier period doubted whether there was any point in returning to the Territory, but new missionaries were sent nonetheless.[18] Numerically, the MEC became the largest *neomejicano* Protestant group in New Mexico during the nineteenth century.

The Harwoods and New Mexican Methodism

Thomas Harwood kept a diary throughout his ministry, which he published as part of his memoirs at the end of his ministry. Emily Harwood's biography was written by Harriet Kellogg in 1903, soon after Emily's death. These documents are important because the Harwoods were the missionaries who remained in the Territory the longest, had a strong impact on New Mexican Methodism, and reflected the general attitudes of Protestant missionaries in the Territory of New Mexico during the nineteenth century.[19]

For the Harwoods and most other Protestant missionaries in New Mexico, Catholicism was the basis of most, if not all, of the "problems" faced by *neomejicanos*. New Mexico was believed to be under the control of priests,[20] who kept the people illiterate, took financial advantage of them and did not allow Protestant missionaries to help them.[21] Catholicism was a faith that "fettered the intellect" of Mexicans. The priests controlled public schools and did not allow *neomejicano* children to learn "the language of Protestants."[22] Because of this, New Mexico "is one of the darkest corners of the world. . . . Romanism . . . culminated over the intellectual skies of the Mexican people and drenched their soil with the polluting floods of Jesuitical traditions, superstitions and ignorance."[23] The only hope for New Mexico's capital, Santa Fe, would be "when the dim candlelight of her Romish altars shall be removed and the bright sun of Protestant Christianity shall arise."[24]

The Harwoods had very negative views of the people with whom they were working. *Neomejicanos* were a "slumbering people"[25] who had little sense of progress. They had been "isolated from the centers of modern civilization, without the advantages of education, without the Bible, without religious freedom," so it was not surprising they were so backward.[26] *Neomejicanos* did not practice hygiene and manners, and although they shared what they had very liberally, Harwood did not like to stay overnight with them because of their unsanitary practices.[27] The people's superstition and their alienation from "civilization" and religious freedom accounted for their rejection of Protestantism and of the Anglo American way of life.[28] The people spoke a "perverted" Spanish,[29] and Mexican women were not very good as "house-help" and could not "cook to suit Americans."[30] Because of this, the work in New Mexico was "foreign in every respect." Nonetheless, Methodists should not ignore the Territory because *neomejicanos* were within the limits of the United States.[31]

The only hope for *neomejicanos*, according to the Harwoods, was for them to accept the Protestant faith, since all of their current problems could be directly attributed to their religious beliefs. "While the march of civilization had taken grand strides, almost everywhere else, New Mexico had fallen behind. Why? For want of Bibles, schools and proper instruction."[32]

Thomas Harwood was particularly proud of *neomejicano* young people who broke the social norms of their society and followed Anglo American mores. When a young lady married an Anglo against her parents' wishes he stated, "this is one of the noble qualities of Protestantism. It is progress. It is Americanism. It is independence. It is surely as it ought to be."[33]

The Harwoods were also concerned about the Anglo Americans migrating into New Mexico who were not living up to the lofty ideals of "Americanism." Because of them, Protestantism's advance was "often wounded in the house of its friends."[34] This army of "immigrating American mendicants and paupers" were making the missionaries' task difficult.[35] The Harwoods often felt that they were the only ones who dared "speak a word against Sabbath breaking, intemperance, gambling, or the dance." The answer for New Mexico was American Protestant civilization, but many Anglo Americans were becoming like the *neomejicanos* instead being examples of what Anglo American civilization had to offer.[36]

According to Thomas Harwood, the missionaries' task was clear. A battle was being waged between Catholicism and Protestantism, and the missionary had to go forward with the biblical message no matter the cost. To retreat would be an injustice to the growing number of *neomejicano* believers. "There must be no retreat. A victory in New Mexico for our holy Christianity, in the name of the King of battles, must be won."[37]

Thomas Harwood described himself as a pioneer and a loner. He often traveled alone (with his Colt revolver), even though it was not considered safe at the time.[38] He was used to making unilateral decisions and not having them questioned. Because of his way of doing things, he would often have accusations raised against him, particularly regarding the use and distribution of funds.[39] Harwood did not feel compelled to follow MEC dictates and limitations. He often intervened personally to obtain more funds for a project than what had been allotted.[40] He spent a great deal of time defending himself at conference sessions, and after official decisions had been taken, he would seek other channels to continue presenting his perspective.[41]

Most Protestant missionary efforts among Mexican Americans in the Southwest had strong leaders, but none of them were as steady and enduring as the MEC's Thomas Harwood in the Territory of New Mexico. Harwood was appointed superintendent of missions in New Mexico in 1872.[42] He was also the first presiding elder of the New Mexico Spanish Mission Conference formed in 1884 and the key leader of its work there until the early twentieth century. Methodists ordained *neomejicano* leaders before the Presbyterians or Congregationalists did, but leadership remained centralized throughout the nineteenth century, largely in Thomas Harwood's hands.

Methodist Mission Efforts and Methods in New Mexico

When the Harwoods arrived in New Mexico, they organized an English-language church in Tiptonville. Through this effort they made contact with Benito García, who became one of Thomas Harwood's early assistants. When Harwood changed his ministry focus to *neomejicanos* he began this new effort by visiting small communities with García at his side.

Santos Telles

Some of the first communities Harwood and García visited were those where Methodists and Baptists had worked in the 1850s. In November 1871 Harwood reorganized the congregation at Peralta, leaving Ambrosio Gonzales in charge of the group that he had been leading since Dalas Lore had assigned him to it in 1855.[43] The group at Socorro was also organized as a Methodist church (1873), with the blessing of one of the former Baptist missionaries (Shaw) and under the leadership of one of the early Baptist lay leaders, Santos Telles.[44] From there Harwood went to Palomas, where the Baptist

Chávez family lived. He organized the Palomas group as a Methodist church in 1873.[45] From this base Harwood and several
neomejicanos licensed as MEC ministers began to expand into
neighboring communities. As Harwood reflected in his diary in
1873, "at that time denominationalism didn't count much."[46] By
1880 there were six Spanish-speaking Methodist congregations
reporting membership in New Mexico.

An important part of the Methodist mission strategy was
the development of *neomejicano* preachers and evangelists. Several of those who worked with Harwood were trained, licensed
to preach, and sent out to work in various parts of the Territory. Harwood argued that, if properly trained, native preachers were better suited for the ministry than missionaries who
had to learn the language and the culture. *Neomejicanos* knew
the territory, comfortably traveled the terrain, and would be
better received by their own people. They would also cost the
MEC mission society less money.[47] Methodists chose to quickly
license *neomejicano* workers (they licensed three by 1875) and
send them out with minimal training.[48]

Harwood's call for training of *neomejicanos* for Methodist
ministry did not mean that he was opposed to Anglo missionaries
entering the Territory. Soon after his arrival he made a written plea
for Methodists to teach Spanish in MEC seminaries.[49] Several
MEC missionaries entered New Mexico to work among the Anglo
American immigrants, and a number also worked among Mexican
Americans. They served as pastors and trainers of the Mexican
American workers, and many of their wives served as teachers (a
part of Methodist missionary strategy). Harwood reports that,
when he organized the congregation at Palomas, the people specifically asked for an Anglo American preacher and a school.[50]

One of the most important tools for extending the Methodist message was circuit riding. Both missionaries and native
workers traveled for weeks at a time, visiting many communities and initiating Sunday school study groups in each. The goal

was for these Sunday schools to eventually develop into churches.[51] A second part of the strategy was to erect church buildings in the communities where new groups were being organized. These were important because Catholics had churches in almost every village in the Territory. If Protestant children were to be retained and new people won, "churches are an important necessity, or we fail to impress them with the superiority and permanency of Protestantism."[52]

MEC home mission policy stipulated that buildings for mission churches were to be constructed with a combination of local funds and a grant from the Board of Church Extension. But Harwood argued that the people were poor and the funds required from the local congregation could not be raised by *neomejicano* congregations or even by many English-language churches in New Mexico. Methodist workers in the Territory requested that New Mexican churches be exempted from the fundraising requirement.[53] It is not clear whether the board granted the request. Harwood sidestepped home mission policy by raising the local congregation's contribution with the help of "several Americans."[54] By 1883 eight of the twelve *neomejicano* congregations had their own buildings.[55]

Thomas Harwood and others in New Mexico also saw the need for literature in New Mexico. As early as 1872 he called for the publication of Methodist books and tracts in Spanish and lamented the fact that the 1880 MEC General Conference did not provide for the publication of literature in Spanish in spite of the opening doors in various Spanish-speaking countries.[56] In 1884 he led the New Mexico Conference to pass a resolution that called on the ME Publishing House to print books in Spanish for "the course of study and the propagation of the gospel of Christ among the Spanish-speaking people."[57] Harwood not only pushed for Spanish-language literature, but also produced his own. He was the editor of at least three different Spanish or bilingual periodicals: the *Metodista Neo-Mexicano*,

El Metodista, and *El Abogado Cristiano.* These were produced for the Spanish-language congregations and also intended to propagate the Protestant faith.

Although Methodists viewed Catholic teachings and practice as false, their mission strategy incorporated Catholic practices that did not contradict their Protestant convictions. For example, although Methodist polity did not have godparents as part of infant baptism, Methodists in New Mexico incorporated it into their practice. The people who stood alongside the parents were called sponsors, but their function mirrored that of godparents, both religiously and socially.[58]

MEC ministry efforts worked on the assumption that missionaries needed a substantial amount of outside support to carry out their work. According to an 1884 conference report, "The native people, so recently breaking away from Romanism, still in the midst of their Roman Catholic enemies and persecutors and very poor, could not be expected to do much toward self-support."[59] The Harwoods often compared their finances to what Presbyterians were receiving or to what the MEC was giving for ministry in Mexico and South America. They felt that their work continued and thrived only because of self-sacrifice.[60]

Yet considering the amount of money invested, the ministry produced strong results. Thomas Harwood often sought to demonstrate that money invested in ministry among the Spanish-speaking communities of New Mexico was producing better results than that being used in other areas, including among the Anglo population of the Territory. For example, in his 1888 report to the New Mexico Conference of the MEC, Harwood stated that he had compared the costs of mission for the Spanish work in New Mexico with the English work in the Territory and with MEC missions in South America and Mexico. He concluded that the Spanish work in New Mexico produced the best per cost ratio between mission expenditures and number of members. Specifically, he stated that "to hold the American members and converts in New Mexico in the same field with the Spanish work has cost the mission funds of the church three times as much as each member of the spanish [*sic*] work."[61]

Harwood was convinced that Methodist efforts had the potential to make *neomejicanos* into Protestants. Protestantism would not only give them a correct relationship with God but would also make them a better people. New Mexico was an "oppressed and priest-ridden country."[62] But in areas such as Peralta—where a significant percentage of the population had become Protestant—one could already see an improvement in the quality of life between those who were Protestant and those who were not, measured in terms of things like higher literacy, better hygiene, and the use of "American" technology.[63]

Methodists and Schools

The Harwoods were convinced that "with the native of this country we must educate in order to Christianize."[64] They were frustrated by the fact that the U.S. government did not establish schools immediately after conquering the Southwest. The Catholic Church was allowed to remain in control in matters of "education, religion and morals," giving the Mexican population the impression "that our nation was a Roman Catholic nation."[65] The U.S. government took forty-five years to establish a fully developed public school system in New Mexico. According to Emily, there were free schools in several Latin American countries before they were established in the Territory.[66] "Had our government, after the treaty of Guadalupe Hidalgo, in 1848, entered this field with the schoolmaster, and encouraged the missionary to enter with an open Bible, as has been done in our New Possessions, how different would have been the results of missionary labor."[67]

Schools were seen as part of a general mission strategy. They were necessary for the children of the Protestant converts who could not be sent to schools controlled by Catholics, or

Protestants would risk losing them.[68] Catholic children also attended Protestant schools, and it was possible "that some of
them may become standard bearers of the cross."[69] Protestant
schools were so successful and accepted by the people that the
Catholic Church started their own schools near them to counteract their influence among the *neomejicano* population.[70]
These schools were also important because they helped remove
"the prejudices of the people so that the establishment of a public school law for New Mexico was passed."[71]

Methodists also considered schools an important part of
church leadership development. Future pastors should be men
who "are in advance of their congregations in education," or mission work would suffer as the new generation of children and
young people became more educated.[72] Good primary schools
would produce knowledgeable men capable of leading a new generation of Christians. And if a good school of "high grade" were
established for leadership development in the territory, it would
be possible to train workers for other parts of the Southwest.[73]

Nonetheless, much to the chagrin of the Harwoods, schools
were never as important for Methodist mission strategy as they
were for the Presbyterians. The Harwoods stated that they could
not compete because the PCUSA spent six dollars on education
for every one spent by the MEC.[74] Hence Presbyterians were able
to set up many more schools and charge lower tuition.[75] Several
Methodist missionaries (including the Harwoods and the Stee-
les) set up small mission schools in the communities where they
were working, often with their wives as teachers. These efforts
often had no outside funding and most were short-lived.

Summary of Methodist Episcopal Church Work in the Territory of New Mexico

The MEC Spanish Mission Conference in the Territory of New
Mexico was the largest of all Spanish-speaking church confer-

ences in the Southwest during the nineteenth century. It experienced steady growth throughout the nineteenth century. A key difference between the MEC and the PCUSA seems to be an important factor in that growth. The MEC had a more dynamic view of leadership and so they licensed *neomejicano* leaders quickly and gave them opportunities to minister. These leaders did not have a great deal of formal training for ministry, but they were mentored and trained while circuit riding with more experienced Anglo leaders. This created a large pool of evangelists who were able to expand the work into many areas beyond the reach of the missionaries sent out by the home mission board.

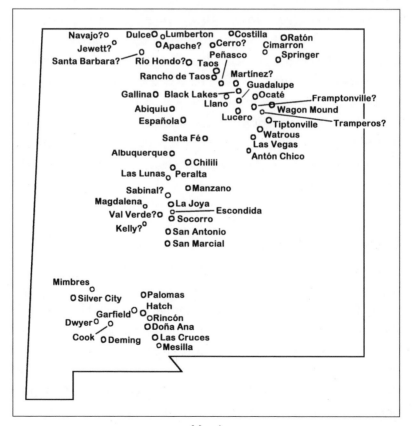

Map 4
Mexican American Methodist Episcopal Church Preaching Appointments, 1900
Territory of New Mexico

Also, because MEC ordination requirements were not as high as those of the PCUSA, a *neomejicano* was ordained in 1877 (Benito García), and many other Mexican Americans soon followed in his footsteps.[76] By 1898 a *neomejicano* was placed in charge of an elder district (J. P. Sánchez).

Another important factor in Methodist growth was the use of the preaching circuits. Methodist evangelists visited many different communities and started Sunday schools wherever they could. Many of these efforts never developed beyond this point, but those that did contributed to a growing number of congregations and steady membership growth throughout most of the nineteenth century.

Nonetheless, the MEC also struggled with developing churches that could not be supported by the *neomejicanos*. They also developed churches in a way that required constant home mission support. Thomas Harwood reasoned that *neomejicanos* were poor and it was difficult for them to contribute in such a situation.[77] And, he insisted, the situation was not as bad as it might seem. Regardless, the economic dependency persisted throughout the nineteenth century and into the twentieth century.

Congregational Church

The third denomination to work in the Spanish-speaking communities of New Mexico after the Civil War was the Congregational Church. Congregational missionaries initiated work with the Spanish-speaking population during the early 1880s. As early as 1882, Jacob Ashley called for people to work with *neomejicanos* and mentioned several communities that had demonstrated interest in the Protestant message (Old Albuquerque, Cabura [Cubero?], San Rafael, and San Mateo).[78] In 1883 he stated that the people of one village were ready to build a church, but lack of leadership and vehement Catholic opposition caused them to give up on the plan. He also mentioned a "good Mexican brother" (Ancheta?) whom he hoped to recruit to be a Congregational worker among *neomejicanos*.[79]

The first meeting of the General Association of Congregational Churches in New Mexico and Arizona included a report by Ashley on "Christian Work among Indians and Mexicans." G. R. Archeta (Ancheta?) was examined and licensed to preach. He led a prayer in Spanish during one of the sessions.[80] The same year, Ashley referred to two schools with Mexican children and mentioned a Mr. Salazar who worked and traveled with him.[81] Charles Sumner, a missionary in New Mexico, wrote several reports for the *Home Missionary*, a Congregationalist publication, in which he referred to the work in Spanish-speaking communities. He made several pleas for more workers and described Ancheta's service, but mentioned no concrete results of the efforts.[82]

The minutes of the 1886 session of the General Association mention that Ancheta and his wife were baptized and that Ancheta was ordained for ministry. A "Chavis" [*sic*] (Ezequiel Chávez?) was licensed. The minutes gave a positive report of the work being done, but no Spanish-speaking churches or concrete results of their labor were mentioned. During the 1888 meeting of the association, Chávez was ordained. He also presented a paper on the "Work among the Mexicans," but no details were given on the content of the effort.[83] The next session at which Spanish-speaking workers were mentioned was in 1890, when Chávez led a devotional.[84]

In 1891 E. Lyman Hood, a Congregationalist missionary in New Mexico, wrote a report on New Mexico and Arizona for the *Home Missionary*, in which he stated that "the work among the native Mexicans is especially urgent and promising at this time." He mentioned that Congregationalists had developed a school to prepare people for work with the Spanish-speaking people. At that point the school had two students and others in view. Hood also reported on a meeting held between workers in Mexico and New Mexico, but the article does not report any specifics abpout the work.[85]

The earliest extant statistical data regarding *neomejicano* Congregationalists is a January 1, 1892, membership list of the First Congregational Church of Albuquerque. The list includes eleven current members with Spanish surnames, including the Rev. E. Chávez. It also mentions four ex-members with Spanish surnames, including Mr. and Mrs. Ancheta, listed as deceased. The church's membership manual includes membership requirements in Spanish. Official conference documents do not record any other statistical data about *neomejicano* Congregationalists during the nineteenth century. Other reports mention work in Spanish-speaking communities, but none give official statistical results, and none of the preaching points are ever listed as officially recognized churches.

Congregationalists had a negative view of Catholics in New Mexico, as can be seen in some of the articles published in *The Home Missionary* by "Mexican missionaries." Several describe the idolatrous practices of the native population.[86] Like other Protestant groups in the Territory, they blamed many of the ills of *neomejicano* society on the Catholic Church. Congregationalists found it difficult to reach Catholics with the gospel and blamed the Catholic Church for keeping the people in spiritual and intellectual darkness. They were especially concerned with the Catholic Church's opposition to public education.[87]

Like the Presbyterians and Methodists, Congregationalists saw education as a means of reaching *neomejicanos* with the Protestant message. The 1886 meeting of the New Mexico Association mentioned fifteen to twenty teachers in Arizona and New Mexico and issued a call for many more to be sent.[88] According to one New Mexican missionary, "The school is the best thing for them. I suppose, when this people get educated, we will have new-born men in this Territory."[89] An 1888 article in *The Home Missionary* states that "when the boys and girls can read good English literature, their minds may be molded in the right way."[90] Congregationalists were not only involved in primary education. Congregationalist Horacio Ladd was crucial in establishing the first University of New Mexico, which functioned from 1881 until 1888 (the state university began in 1889). Ladd said this university was needed because "of its peculiar situation within our own borders, among a native foreign people using the Spanish language, and where the Roman Catholic religion is supreme in its control of the legislation and the consciences of the great majority of the inhabitants."[91] Ladd called upon Congregationalists in the East to support the university because it would be distinctively Protestant and Christian in its charter and management.[92] Its education would secure Christian character in its students and positively influence New Mexico.

Congregationalists never reported established churches among *neomejicanos* during the nineteenth century. First Ancheta and then Chávez reported preaching points that Randi Walker refers to as congregations.[93] Reports written by the Congregationalist superintendent Jacob Ashley and Chávez mention six communities.[94] Both Ancheta and Chávez report drawing several people together whenever they preached in these communities, as did Ashley. But few of these people ever became members of a Congregational Church.

As late as 1892, *neomejicano* Congregationalist leaders (such as Ezequiel Chávez) were listed as members of the Albuquerque Congregational Church. The eleven people listed in the 1892 church report are the only *neomejicanos* clearly identified as members of a Congregational Church in conference records.[95] Later reports seem to confirm that Congregationalist work among *neomejicanos* never produced many committed members or strong congregations. In 1909 there were only two Spanish-language congregations listed among the Congregational Churches of the New Mexico Association.[96] The small number is due, at least in part, to the fact that there were never many Anglo Congregationalists in New Mexico either. The 1909 association minutes list only six churches in the entire territory.[97] Because of this, there were never many Congregationalist missionaries among *neomejicanos*.

American Baptist Convention

The American Baptist Convention (BAP), which did the most work in the Territory of New Mexico before the Civil War, did not reestablish itself in *neomejicano* communities until the beginning of the twentieth century. As stated earlier, most of the people who had become Baptists during the 1850s became a part of MEC congregations, although a few apparently maintained a strong Baptist identity.[98]

Protestantism Among *Neomejicanos* in 1900

In 1900 nearly half the Spanish-speaking Protestant population in the United States was in the Territory of New Mexico. The 2,521 *neomejicano* Protestants constituted forty-five percent of all Spanish-speaking adult Protestant church members in the Southwest. The largest Protestant denomination among Mexican Americans in the Territory was the MEC (sixty-one percent), followed by the PCUSA (thirty-seven percent) and the Congregationalists (two percent) (Graph 2).

Factors Making Protestantism Attractive to Neomejicanos

Many *neomejicanos* were dissatisfied with the Catholic Church. The Catholic hierarchy had largely ignored the area when it was under Mexican control, and when U.S. Catholics assumed

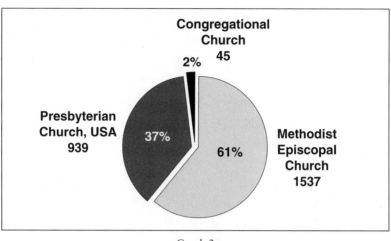

Graph 2
Mexican American Protestants, 1900
Territory of New Mexico

leadership they sent the unpopular French bishop Lamy, who excommunicated several priests, including the popular José Antonio Martínez, and alienated the people as described before. Also, when Protestant missionaries arrived, few schools existed in the Territory. *Neomejicanos* saw the need for their children's education and were willing to send their offspring to Protestant schools—if they were the only ones available—even against the wishes of local priests. These schools did not produce many direct converts, but they did accomplish several things. Because most of the teachers were females, the schools provided a setting where Protestant workers could make contact with Spanish-speaking people without strong opposition. Many *neomejicanos* heard the Protestant message through missionary teachers. The schools also served as safe haven for the children of Protestant church members and as an early training ground for second-generation Protestant leaders. The schools also functioned as doorways into U.S. society. Parents who wanted their children to fit into U.S. society often sent them to Protestant schools, although they usually did not want them to become Protestants.

Barriers Between Protestants and Neomejicanos

The Protestant missionaries were convinced that Anglo American civilization was Christian and superior so they were very ethnocentric. Since their culture was better, anything that was not "American" was inferior. Because of this mindset, the missionaries saw very little need to study and understand *neomejicano* culture. Their goal was to prove that Protestantism and its cultural manifestation "Americanism" were superior and to convince the people to become Protestant Americans. Some missionaries showed curiousity toward the local customs, but few saw value in them.

This attitude was also common toward the converts. They were not treated as equals, partners in a common religious confession. If becoming a Protestant was supposed to open the door to U.S. society, it seldom worked in the nineteenth century. Most Protestants "adopted the prevailing prejudices against the Spanish-speaking people which relegated them to second-class citizenship."[99]

The missionaries' anti-Catholicism also kept them from understanding the nature of *neomejicano* relations with the Roman Catholic Church. They accurately assessed that *neomejicanos* were frustrated with the Catholic Church, but they misunderstood the nature of their frustration. The missionaries preached against Catholic beliefs and what they perceived as control by the priests. Yet the early converts were drawn to Protestantism for different reasons. A very crucial issue was pastoral support. During the early years Protestant missionaries were most successful in the areas where there were few priests.[100] Once the Catholic Church began sending more priests into *neomejicano* communities this initial interest in Protestantism was lost.

A related issue had to do with the *Penitentes*. Some early *Penitente* leaders were open to the Protestant message because it addressed two crucial issues for them: spiritual vitality and freedom to have their own leaders. *Penitente* leaders found spaces as Bible study leaders and lay evangelists in Protestant churches, while the Catholic Church was trying to proscribe their influence. Nonetheless, the Protestant missionaries interpreted these conversions primarily as a recognition that Protestantism was superior to Catholicism, not as a specific response to actions to a Catholic Church that was not meeting their spiritual needs.

Missionaries in New Mexico also faced the fact that foreign mission boards enthusiastically sent missionaries and support to Mexico and Latin America, but did not express the same interest in ministry to Spanish-speaking *neomejicanos*. Several missionaries in New Mexico publicly lamented this paradox and the limitations it placed on their ministry: "Note the unfailing enthusiasm that missions in Mexico always awaken; contrast this with the apathy shown toward substantially the same work, among the same people, only on the United States' side of the geographical line that separates this republic from that of Mexico."[101]

Home mission societies were also concerned with the westward-bound Anglo American and European immigrants and several worked among Native Americans and African Americans. Foreign mission societies focused on Mexico and Latin America. Hence, the Spanish-speaking people of the Southwest never attracted the interest or response given to other groups.

There were also inherent contradictions among the various goals of Protestant missionaries in New Mexico. On the one hand they wanted to establish strong churches to reach the *neomejicano* population. On the other hand, the missionaries wanted to "Americanize" Mexican Americans. This usually meant that the *neomejicanos* most interested in assimilating into Anglo American culture were those most attracted to Protestantism. Many of these people were alienated from their own communities and could not serve as a strong base from which to attract *neomejicanos* who were not so interested in assimilation. And Mexican Americans who "Americanized" no longer wanted to be a part of *neomejicano* institutions. Protestant missionaries apparently never realized that they could not both successfully Americanize *neomejicano* converts and establish strong *neomejicano* Protestant churches.

The people of northern New Mexico had lived in small, isolated communities for several centuries before the Anglo Americans arrived. These communities were stable and had pastoral economies that adequately met the needs of the population. But when the Anglo Americans arrived, they changed the economic structures and built new communities where they concentrated the new economic power. The small towns of northern New Mexico were left isolated, with little possibility of growth. Many were eventually abandoned.

Numerous Protestant churches were started in these small rural communities of northern New Mexico. There was little chance that these churches would ever be very large or become stable congregations. As the United States economy imposed itself on New Mexico, traditional ways of earning a living began to disappear. Families who had lived in one place for generations became part of the newly disposable labor force, looking for employment wherever they could find it. Thomas Harwood reports that MEC congregations lost members as people left for California, Arizona, and even Oklahoma. One of the most extreme losses occurred in Deming, where a new congregation migrated, *en toto*, to California.[102]

Beginnings of a Neomejicano Protestant Identity

Nonetheless, *neomejicano* Protestants begin to develop their own ethno-religious identity. They saw themselves as a new generation of Reformers who would bring change to the Catholic Church that was so much a part of *neomejicano* life. *Neomejicano* Protestants also became the leaders of their local congregations and found spaces where they could develop as leaders. These converts also began identifying key symbols of their new identity. The proscribed *Penitentes* venerated Padre Martínez. But so did *neomejicano* Presbyterians, who saw him as a voice for reform and an indirect spiritual ancestor, through Vicente Romero and his descendents. The Bible also became a crucial symbol for these converts. They found truth through the Bible and they developed a folklore about the role and importance of the Bible in *neomejicano* Protestant life.[103]

Protestant churches continued to grow during the first years of the twentieth century, but then they began to disappear. By the 1920s *neomejicano* MEC, PCUSA, and Congregationalist churches suffered a downturn from which they never recovered, particularly in northern New Mexico.[104] *Neomejicano* continued becoming Protestants, but most growth occurred in southern New Mexico. And growing numbers of *neomejicanos* were attracted to the new movement called Pentecostalism, including many who had previously been Methodists or Presbyterians.

7

"Doing What He Could"

MEXICAN AMERICAN PROTESTANTISM
IN COLORADO, THE TERRITORY
OF ARIZONA, AND CALIFORNIA

---

*People say the Mexican is a Roman Catholic, and there-
fore some kind of a Christian. These people are no more
nor less than idolatrous, the very best of them.*
                                    Alexander Darley (1880)

*[They need the] right kind of men to lead them . . . a pru-
dent, intelligent Methodist missionary who can speak the
Spanish language, and teach and preach in their own
tongue.*
                        Methodist Episcopal Church [Southern]
                                    California Conference (1881)

MOST NINETEENTH-CENTURY MEXICAN AMERICAN PROTESTANTS
lived in New Mexico or Texas. Colorado had a much smaller
Spanish-speaking Protestant population, and there were only
five Latino congregations in Arizona and three in California. By
1900 only twelve percent of all reported Mexican American

Protestants in the Southwest lived in Colorado, Arizona, and California combined.

Colorado

The region of Colorado where most Spanish-speaking people lived had been a part of Spanish and Mexican *Nuevo Méjico* and was included in the original delineation of the U.S. Territory of New Mexico. Most of the people in the San Luis Valley of southern Colorado originally migrated from New Mexico and maintained close ties with northern New Mexico. These ties were reflected in Protestant ministry efforts. MEC work in Colorado had a New Mexican base. PCUSA efforts in Colorado and New Mexico were officially separate but made use of several joint efforts in their work with the Spanish-speaking communities of the two regions.

Presbyterian Church in the United States of America

PCUSA work among Mexican Americans in southern Colorado apparently began in New Mexico. Pablo Ortega, a *Penitente* leader from Cenicero, Colorado, converted to Protestantism while in Santa Fe under the PCUSA missionary D. F. McFarland. His brother-in-law, Pedro Sánchez, bought a Bible (at considerable cost), which became the focus of a Bible study group that included Sánchez, the Ortega brothers, and others. When PCUSA missionaries James Roberts of New Mexico and Alexander Darley, working in Colorado, began working together in southern Colorado, they encountered this homegrown Bible study group and organized it into a PCUSA church in Cenicero (1876). Most Presbyterian churches organized in southern Colorado (and Costilla, New Mexico) trace their origins to this Bible study group.

The second congregation began in a similar fashion. Juan

Gómez bought a Bible in the 1860s and took it with him when he migrated into southern Colorado. He and his family began reading and discussing the Bible together and developed a Bible study that included neighbors and even a local priest. When Alexander Darley heard about the group, he visited them and soon afterward organized them into the Presbyterian Church of La Luz (1879).[1]

Several early Mexican American converts became lay evangelists who spread the Protestant message among the people of the San Luis Valley. Due to their efforts, churches were started in several communities.

Most early Mexican American Protestants in southern Colorado ended up at the margin of their communities after their conversion. Protestant marginalization was particularly pronounced in three villages in the San Luis Valley. Tensions between Protestants and Catholics in these villages led to a climate of mistrust and fear. The villages eventually split down religious lines and new towns were established. The new "twin" communities were: Costilla, New Mexico (Protestant) and García, Colorado (Catholic); San Pablo (Protestant) and San Pedro (Catholic); and Mogote (Protestant) and San Rafael (Catholic).[2]

Most Mexican American Protestant leadership formation in the nineteenth century was informal; leaders developed through mentoring relationships with missionaries. At the end of the nineteenth century, several small training programs were developed, but most were short-lived. The only college program developed during the nineteenth century to train Mexican American pastors was the Presbyterian College of the Southwest at Del Norte, Colorado. The institution began as a general education college in 1884, largely due to the efforts of George Darley (Alexander Darley's brother). The college had general education programs for both English- and Spanish-speaking students.[3]

In 1890 Francis Gilchrist of New Mexico recommended that the college begin a program for Mexican American evangelists.

Several young leaders from southern Colorado and northern New Mexico were sent to study there. The college continued its general education program, but shifted its focus to training pastors and colporteurs to work in the Spanish-speaking communities of the Southwest. In 1893 the first group of students graduated from the three-year program for ministers. That first class included several key future Mexican American leaders of New Mexico and southern Colorado, such as M. D. J. Sánchez and Gabino Rendón. Amadeo Maés, Refugio Jaramillo, and Juan Quintana were part of the second graduating class. Other well-known graduates were Manuel Madrid and J. J. Vigil.[4]

Unfortunately the college did not have a strong financial base and depended on outside subsidies. A small gold rush created an economic boom in the Del Norte area, but it was short-lived. Most of school's students were poor and could pay little for their education. Several students were married and needed to support their families. Because of the lack of funds, the col-

First graduates (1893) of the Theological Class, Presbyterian College of the Southwest. Standing, left to right: Manual Madrid, José Vigil, Gabriel Sánchez, Warren Buell; seated, left to right: Gabino Rendón, R. E. Hays, Professor Francis Gilchrist, Abelino Aguirre, Luis Bernal.

lege closed in 1901.[5] This was a serious blow to PCUSA work in the Spanish-speaking communities, as it had been the principal training ground for Presbyterian pastors and leaders. Several years after its closure, a survey was done of forty of its Spanish-speaking graduates. The survey showed that "8 had become ordained ministers, 10 were evangelists, 9 were teachers, 4 were editors, 4 were ministers' wives, 3 were merchants, 1 was a lawyer, and 1 was in the employ of the government."[6]

When the Pueblo Presbytery held its first meeting in 1881, it included three pastors from Spanish-speaking churches in the San Luis Valley. The number grew to five by 1885 but then decreased to three in 1888. New churches were planted in 1893, partially because of the work of Del Norte College graduates. Students and graduates from Del Norte were assigned to various communities in southern Colorado and worked under the supervision of Anglo professors or missionaries. Congregations were established throughout the region during the 1890s. By 1900 there were fourteen Spanish-language PCUSA churches in southern Colorado. Mexican American students or alumni of Del Norte led most of them.

The population of the San Luis Valley in southern Colorado was not large. Most of the communities were small, and the churches established in those communities were also small. From 1878 to 1892, six congregations were established; by 1892 only four were still in existence with a total of ninety-nine adult church members. By 1900 only one church had over fifty members (San Rafael). The congregations had an average membership of twenty-nine, making them smaller than their counterparts in New Mexico. Four had fewer than twenty members.[7]

Methodist Episcopal Church

MEC missionary work in the San Luis Valley of southern Colorado began in the late 1880s as an extension of MEC ministry

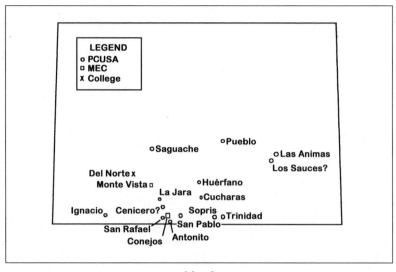

Map 5
Mexican American Methodist Episcopal Church
and Presbyterian Church, USA Churches, 1900
Colorado

in New Mexico. The first congregation, Conejos, was organized in 1889. Three other preaching appointments were reported in 1894, but only two continued into 1895 (Monte Vista
and San Luis). From 1896 to 1900, the New Mexico Spanish
Mission Conference reported two congregations, Conejos and
Monte Vista. MEC work in Colorado was never very strong
and church membership remained unstable.

Overview of Mexican American Protestantism
in Colorado

The Spanish-speaking population of southern Colorado was
small and located in isolated communities. Protestant efforts reflected that reality. By 1900 there were 462 members in the sixteen Mexican American Protestant churches in the state (Map
5). The majority, 89 percent (410), were Presbyterians and the
rest were Methodists (52).[8] Two-thirds of all Mexican Ameri-

can Protestant church members in Colorado in 1900 had converted after 1892.

Protestant growth in southern Colorado during the nineteenth century depended on several key factors. When the first
Presbyterian missionaries arrived, they found people who were already studying the Bible and were open to the Protestant message.
The first two congregations in the state both resulted from Bible
studies initiated by local Mexican Americans before the missionaries arrived. Understandably, the Bibles used by these groups
gained legendary status among Mexican American Presbyterians.[9]

The first known Mexican American Protestant in the area,
Pablo Sánchez, was a former *Penitente* leader. The single most
significant factor in the growth of Protestantism in southern
Colorado, however, was the Presbyterian College of the Southwest, particularly after 1893, when the first Mexican Americans graduated. Students trained in this college started new
churches in Colorado, and several were crucial in PCUSA work
among Mexican Americans in other parts of the Southwest during the early twentieth century.

As MEC work in New Mexico grew stronger, it began to
expand beyond its borders. MEC work in Colorado was a direct result of New Mexico Spanish Mission Conference ministry expansion. Although MEC efforts in southern Colorado
were never strong during the nineteenth century, they were possible because the churches in New Mexico were expanding.

Despite these factors favorable to Protestant efforts, there
were never many Mexican American Protestants in southern
Colorado during the nineteenth century, and the few churches
established in the state never grew significantly. This can be attributed to several factors. The Mexican American communities
of southern Colorado were located in very isolated areas. The
state was experiencing rapid growth, and even the community
of Del Norte, not far from most of the Mexican American
churches, enjoyed a small economic boom. Most of the congre-

gations, however, were in isolated rural towns that had little possibility of growth. Protestants could not establish stable churches in economically unstable communities.

The three twin Catholic-Protestant communities in the area demonstrate the tension and separation that existed between Mexican American Protestants and Catholics. The Protestant message called people to separate themselves from their families and communities and to adopt a new culture. New converts became isolated from the rest of the population, making it difficult for them to have an impact on their friends and neighbors.

Anti-Catholicism was a common thread among all Protestant missionaries in the Southwest. In southern Colorado its most prominent spokesperson was Alexander Darley, who published the two Spanish-language PCUSA periodicals that circulated in the late nineteenth century. The attacks could be quite strong and further exacerbated the tensions between Catholics and Protestants in the Mexican American communities of the state.[10]

Territory of Arizona

Most of the work among Mexican Americans in Arizona during the nineteenth century also began as an extension of ministries in New Mexico. From their bases in New Mexico, both the PCUSA and the MEC sent workers to the Territory of Arizona. The only exception was a lone MECS church in Phoenix that had ties with MECS work in Mexico.

Presbyterian Church, USA

The PCUSA first reported a Spanish-language church in Arizona in 1881. A licensed *neomejicano* evangelist served as its pastor. Over the next three years, up to five congregations were reported with a membership high of seventy in 1883. But the churches soon lost this early growth and by 1885 statistical reports listed only two churches with a total of twenty-five members. The membership continued to decline, and by 1892, only one PCUSA congregation (Morence) remained open in the Territory. In 1893 Presbyterians established new churches in Florence and Tucson. The congregations in Morence, Florence, and Tucson reported steady membership growth through 1897. In 1898, only Florence reported membership, and in 1899 and 1900 no membership was reported for any Spanish-language Presbyterian Churches in Arizona.[11] Presbyterian work among Mexican Americans in Arizona essentially started over again in 1901.[12]

Methodist Episcopal Church

The MEC began work in the Territory of Arizona late in the century. It reported its first preaching point, Solomonville, in 1891. It was linked with the MEC congregation in Silver City, New Mexico. A second appointment was added in Tucson in 1892. MEC evangelists from New Mexico were assigned to these young congregations, which were seen as an extension of the work in the Territory of New Mexico rather then as a separate ministry effort. These two congregations reported overall growth during their first five years of existence. In 1899 preaching appointments were also reported in Wilcox, Bisbee, and Yuma, though only the latter reported any membership. The MEC also reported erratic growth among Mexican Americans in Arizona. In 1896 the congregations reported 157 members, but by 1900 the same congregations had only 59 members.[13]

Methodist Episcopal Church, South

Mexican American MECS work in Phoenix is first mentioned in an 1891 statistical report of the Northwest Mexican Conference, which included Spanish-language congregations in Texas (El Paso, Ft. Davis, and La Luz), an English-language congregation in Arizona (Nogales), and churches in northwestern Mexico. Emeterio Quiñones, a presiding elder in the conference, and J. J. Mercado, who also pastored an MECS church in Laredo, led the Phoenix congregation during the 1890s. No other Mexican American MECS congregations were established in the territory during the nineteenth century, although workers were assigned to Tucson in 1890 and 1897.

Overview of Mexican American Protestantism in the Territory of Arizona

Protestant mission work among Mexican Americans in Arizona grew erratically during the nineteenth century. In 1897 three denominations reported a membership total of 306 in six congregations. By 1900 only the MEC and MECS reported membership, with 97 members in four congregations (the MEC also reported two congregations with no members). The MEC churches had 59

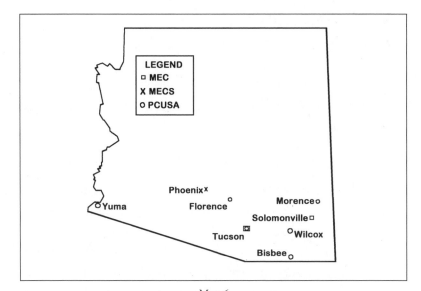

Map 6
Mexican American Methodist Episcopal Church, Methodist Episcopal
Church, South, and Presbyterian Church, USA Churches, 1980–1900
Territory of Arizona

members, and the one MECS congregation had 37 members. The Mexican American congregations were dispersed throughout the southern part of the territory. Two were located in the silver mining areas of eastern Arizona, where the mines employed many Mexican immigrants. Two were in Tucson and the others were in Phoenix, Florence, Yuma, Wilcox, and Bisbee (Map 6).

California

Nineteenth-century Protestants devoted very little energy to working among Mexican Americans in the Golden State. Two Protestant mission agencies worked in various Spanish-speaking communities of the state during the 1800s. The MEC abandoned its efforts after a few years, and the PCUSA built upon the work the former had started. In 1900 California had the smallest number of Spanish-speaking Protestants of any state in the Southwest.

Methodist Episcopal Church

The MEC began ministry among several ethnic minorities in California after the end of the Civil War. By 1868 the denomination was working among the Chinese and German communities, and during the 1870s they sent missionaries to the Native Americans, the Portuguese, and a number of Scandinavian groups.[14] There had been some initial missionary contacts among *californios* in the 1850s,[15] but no official efforts were begun until 1879, when the Northern California Conference asked the denomination to consider the possibility of establishing work among the Spanish-speaking population.[16] The MEC took no further action in Northern California, but the (Southern) California Conference initiated work among Mexican Americans the following year.

In 1880 the MEC began working in the Los Angeles area under the leadership of Antonio Díaz and his wife. The couple was presented to the 1880 Annual (Southern) California Conference, and a strong motion was passed to support them in this new work.[17] In 1881 conference reports on the work were very enthusiastic. An extensive account of Díaz's ministry in Los Angeles reported that he was also working in Anaheim and Azusa.[18] The conference also received an expansive chronicle of the efforts of a Juan B. Martínez, who had started a mission in Santa Barbara. Martínez was highly praised by the representative of the Santa Barbara District.[19] The conference voted to seek funds to establish a superintendent for the Spanish mission.[20]

The 1882 conference reports present mixed results. The (Southern) California Conference statistical report does not mention a membership total for either Los Angeles or Santa Barbara (the national statistical report does list membership for Los Angeles). The report about Díaz states that "our Mexican missionary has been doing what he could among the Spanish-speaking people of the district."[21] He reportedly established congregations in Los Angeles, Los Nietos, Anaheim, Azusa, and El Puente, with a total of 126 members or active participants.[22]

News about Martínez was much more negative. "The missionary [Martínez] exerted his influence with his people during the year, in an special manner, in favor of the 'Band,' rather than in favor of the Church," to such an extent that few would attend the Santa Barbara church's regular services. The report stated that the people needed the "right kind of men to lead them." There was a call to find "a prudent, intelligent Methodist missionary who can speak the Spanish language, and teach and preach in their own tongue."[23]

By 1883 no one reported any work in Los Angeles, and the Santa Barbara district report mentioned the need of a missionary. If funds could not be raised to support a worker, the work would be surrendered "to other Churches who seem more awake to the importance of the Spanish work, or [they will have to] leave them [the Spanish speaking] in the darkness of superstition."[24] MEC ministry efforts among Mexican Americans ended by 1884 and there was no other mention of possible work among Spanish-speaking communities in California until 1889.[25] Methodists never gave any conference report explaining the termination of their work in Los Angeles and Santa Barbara, and the MEC did not resume work among Mexican Americans in California until after 1900.

Presbyterian Church, USA

There were several Anglo Presbyterians in Mexican California, but little is known of any work they may have done among *californios*. A Dr. Willey started a "Sabbath-School" in the presidio at Monterey, apparently for Mexican children, but there is no mention of the outcome of this work or of any other efforts prior to the mid-1880s.[26]

The MEC's termination of its work among Mexican Americans in Los Angeles marked the beginning of PCUSA ministry in the same area. Antonio Díaz disappeared from Methodist reports after 1882 but was listed as a licentiate in the Presbytery of Los Angeles in 1883.[27] Neither Methodist nor Presbyterian records of the period explain Díaz's change of affiliation. According to the Presbyterian historian Eduard Wicher, Díaz was converted to Presbyterianism in Mexico in 1862 before migrating to Los Angeles.[28] Whatever the reason for Díaz's change of denominational affiliation, he apparently took his "converts" with him, as can be seen by comparing the last MEC reports on Mexican American churches and membership totals with the subsequent Spanish language Presbyterian congregations.[29] Díaz was apparently a committed evangelist and preacher who led several key people to conversion. At least four congregations owed their existence to his work.

In 1882 Carlos Bransby, a former missionary to Colombia, was commissioned by the PCUSA home mission board to work with Mexican Americans in the Los Angeles Presbytery. That same year Díaz was licensed as a Presbyterian minister (and ordained in 1884). Under Bransby's leadership, three groups started by Díaz in Anaheim, Los Angeles, and Los Nietos were organized into churches. The Los Angeles congregation closed in 1885 and was restarted in 1889. The church in Anaheim also closed in 1887 and its members were incorporated into the English-language congregation there.

Moss Merwin, a former PCUSA missionary to Chile, arrived in the Los Angeles Presbytery in 1888. He reorganized the church in Los Angeles in 1889 and started congregations in Azusa and San Gabriel in 1891. Presbyterians did not organize any other Spanish-language congregations in California during the nineteenth century. In 1894 the PCUSA also opened a school for Mexican American children in the Los Angeles area. The PCUSA Women's Home Missionary Society supported the institution and a Miss Ida Boone taught there.[30]

During the nineteenth century, PCUSA work among Mexican Americans in California never advanced very far beyond its MEC beginnings. Membership growth was slow, with the only significant growth surge occurring when Moss Merwin organized two new churches in 1889. When Antonio Díaz died in 1895, the church at Los Nietos closed. The other three congregations continued growing under Merwin's leadership and had 115 members in 1900.[31] Presbyterian Church, USA work among Mexican Americans advanced slowly until the twentieth century when the 1910 Mexican Revolution caused thousands of Mexicans to flee to the Los Angeles area. The massive migration provided the impetus for a new surge in Presbyterian ministry among the Spanish speaking in California.

Methodist Episcopal Church, South

Methodist historian Clarence Lokey states that the MECS initiated work in Spanish-speaking communities of California in

1895, but MECS minutes for Southern California never refer to
this work or to any other ministry efforts among Mexican
Americans in California during the nineteenth century.[32]

Overview of Mexican American Protestantism in California

As the nineteenth century drew to a close, California was home
to 115 adult Mexican American Protestants. The three congregations were located in Southern California. The *californio*
population was not very large at the time of the U.S. conquest,
no more than 13,000,[33] and there were not many immigrants
from Mexico or Mexican Americans from other parts of the
Southwest. Nonetheless, Mexican American Protestantism in
California was tied to migration. Antonio Díaz was an immigrant from Mexico and at the close of the nineteenth century
Mexican American Protestants from other parts of the Southwest took their faith with them to California. The Mexican
American communities in California began to grow during the
first part of the twentieth century and it was then that Mexican
American Protestantism in the state began to expand.

8

"A Power for the Uplifting of the Mexican Race"

CHARACTERISTICS OF THE NINETEENTH-CENTURY MEXICAN AMERICAN PROTESTANT COMMUNITY

———◆•❈•◆———

What will the end of this people be under the grasp of the priestly power if such as have light do not come to their rescue with the freedom of the Gospel?
José Ynés Perea (1902)

These . . . stories, along with many individual experiences to be met with among the Mexican people, prove that unlearned and ignorant men are frequently led to a change of heart and life by the "open Bible," even without the preacher. They also prove afresh that the open Bible is ever the foe of Romish superstition.
Francis Gilchrist (1897)

Protestant Spanish-Americans are probably closer to being assimilated into American culture, but in a situation where race prejudice prevents them really becoming identified with the dominant group, especially those in the low-income class.
Carolyn Zeleny (1974)

PROTESTANT MISSIONARY REPORTS TOLD THE STORY OF THE MIS-
sionaries' efforts. They seldom wrote about the converts themselves, except as case studies or as "trophies" demonstrating the
missionaries' success. These descriptions tended to focus on the
religious characteristics of Mexican American Protestants,
though they also often spoke with pride of how "American"
they were becoming. The missionaries sometimes spoke badly of
the converts, but usually in the context of explaining why their
work was so difficult. Toward the end of the nineteenth century
a few missionaries even made a few comments about the socio-
economic conditions of the Mexican Americans, but this was
also usually related to an apology for the limited results.

A few nineteenth-century converts wrote about themselves,
but overall the extant material keeps us from drawing broad
conclusions. Nonetheless, one can define some concrete characteristics of this new ethno-relgious community, charactistics
common among Latino Protestants to this day. Mexican American Protestants were developing a new identity around their
experiences related to their newfound faith.

Evangelistic Enthusiasm

Almost all early Mexican American Protestant leaders had
strong conversion experiences that persuaded them to accept
the Protestant message. Some, like the former *Penitentes*, had
been committed Catholics, but most had not found spiritual
nourishment in the religion of their birth.[1] They were attracted
to what they saw as vitality in Protestantism and, apparently,
few ever returned to Catholicism.[2] These converts' personal experiences persuaded them that their own people also needed to
hear the Protestant message. They preached to their neighbors
and when they could often traveled great distances to find
people interested in listening to their message.

This commitment was particularly pronounced among the

Mexican American preachers. Many were circuit riders, travelling from town to town, ranch to ranch—often for weeks at a time—to find people who wanted to study the Bible. They were motivated by their new convictions and by a deep concern for their people. One of those preachers, José Ynés Perea, wrote a series of articles in the Presbyterian paper *La Aurora* that presented the history of the church in a way that implies that the *neomejicano* Protestant preachers were new reformers following the example of Calvin and Luther and preaching to free their people from the Catholic Church's control.[3] From the perspective of these preachers, if Mexican Americans would hear and accept the Protestant message, they would find new life and spiritual vitality.

The social pressure or persecution that Mexican American leaders suffered at the hands of the Catholic majority only served to persuade these early converts that the Catholic hierarchy wanted to control the people and that they were suffering for the sake of the gospel. Their enthusiasm and self-assurance were so great they occasionally challenged Roman Catholic priests to public debates.[4]

Mexican American Protestants continued in their commitment, in spite of opposition, because they had a sense that God's spirit was guiding and empowering them. Pablo García, an early MECS pastor and historian, reports that during the early years Methodists in Texas and Mexico had a sense that they were all constantly filled with the *"Espíritu del Maestro"* (Spirit of the Master).[5]

Isolation from the Larger Mexican American Community

Nineteenth-century Mexican American Protestants were a minority within a minority. The fact that they had left Catholicism separated them from other Mexican Americans. But because they were Mexican Americans their Anglo Protestant coreligion-

ists did not always readily accept them. Three nineteenth-century Mexican American Protestants, Rodríguez, Perea, and
Rendón, published testimonials about their experiences. All
three relate tensions that developed within their families and
communities when they chose Protestantism.[6] The most extreme
cases of isolation and separation were those reported in northern New Mexico and southern Colorado. For example, the Presbyterian Church of El Rito (Chacón, New Mexico) was organized after several Protestant families migrated from Chamisal
and other communities to a new location to escape Catholic persecution. John Annin found them near Chacón and organized
them into a church.[7] And, as stated earlier, three communities in
southern Colorado split into Catholic and Protestant sections.

Mexican American Protestants also maintained an attitude
of superiority that distanced them from their Catholic communities. They believed they had received the truth, which not only
gave them a personal relationship with God, it also gave them
a better way of life than that of their Catholic relatives and
neighbors. This view is reflected in documents commenting on
the better appearance, cleanliness, and greater intelligence of
Mexican American Protestants.[8]

This isolation was also clearly a result of the Protestant
message, which called for an individual decision in the midst of
a communal society. Protestantism was often most attractive to
Mexican Americans who were already on the fringes of their
communities.[9] Their further alienation reinforced their decision
to become Protestants, since they were now suffering for their
decision to follow Jesus Christ.

Assimilationist Tendencies

After the U.S. takeover, Mexican Americans in the Southwest
were obligated to decide how to relate to the conquering civilization. Some chose to fight, others left to Mexico, and the ma-

jority simply attempted to continue living as they had always lived. But there were also people who reacted positively to the Anglo American presence. They felt that the "American way of life" offered improvement for themselves and their community, and they wanted to become a part of it. Since acceptance of the Protestant message was considered one of the ways to gain access to the "American" lifestyle, many Mexican American Protestants were of this latter type (though many did not seem to have this as a significant motivating factor). Some early converts demonstrated an attraction to Anglo American culture before they became Protestants. For example, both José Perea and Santiago ("James") Tafolla studied in U.S. colleges. Perea and Gabino Rendón both married Anglo missionary teachers. José ("Polly") Rodríguez had been working alongside Americans for several years before becoming a Protestant.

Gabino Rendón

A number of early converts in New Mexico, including Vicente Romero and Gabino Rendón, joined Protestant churches after attending missionary schools. According to Thomas Harwood, Mexican Americans who sent their children to these schools had "caught the spirit of progress and are desirous of bettering their condition, educating their children and placing them on a plane with Americans."[10] These individuals saw an American Protestant education as a way of helping their children fit into the new social order.

Toward the end of the nineteenth century, the Spanish-language churches of New Mexico began losing some of their most educated young people. As the youth gained an education primarily in English, many chose to leave Spanish-language congregations and join English-language churches. At the beginning of the twentieth century, Emily Harwood attributed the slow growth of *neomejicano* MEC churches to the fact that many converts were becoming "educated and Americanized" and opting to join "American" churches.[11]

Loyalty to Protestant Political Views

It is difficult to determine how Mexican American Protestants felt about specific political issues. But at various times during the nineteenth century some missionaries felt it important to be able to affirm that the converts were "good Americans." This tendency was particularly pronounced among the MEC in New Mexico. Both Thomas Harwood's memoirs and Emily Harwood's biography make reference to the fact that *neomejicano* Methodists were "loyal to our government." As stated earlier, during the Civil War three early converts from the Peralta area served in the Union Army.[12] And as the century came to a close, Emily Harwood observed that the converts were "loyal to the core" during the war with Spain (1898). Harriet Kellogg quotes Emily:

> Their sympathies run deep for the suffering Cubans and their patriotism high for our national honor in the war with Spain. Let every Christian pray for the triumph of our arms. . . . We have some 25 Mexican ordained Methodist preachers in this mission who would like to go in the US Army as chaplains in the war for Cuba's independence.[13]

Tenous U.S. Identity

Throughout the nineteenth century the Mexicans of the Southwest were treated as foreigners. They might be U.S. citizens, but they were not "Americans." This also applied to the Protestant converts. Toward the end of the nineteenth century some Protestant missionaries began to distinguish between *neomejicanos* and immigrants from Mexico. But in the rest of the Southwest the people were called Mexicans, no matter where they were born. Even though the converts were supposed to Americanize, the Protestant leadership saw them as outsiders. This new ethnoreligious community was forming its identity with an unclear national identity. They were U.S. citizens and Protestants. But even the Protestant missionaries identified them as Mexicans.

Socio-economic Challenges

Mexican American Protestants were isolated from their own communities and tied religiously to Anglo American Protestants who were part of the new socio-economic order. But their new religion did not exempt them from the pressures Mexican Americans faced because of the structural changes occurring in their communities due to the new social, political, and economic situation. After the U.S. takeover large numbers of Mexican Americans, including Mexican American Protestants, became migrants, members of the U.S. economy's disposable work force.[14] Emily Harwood stated that "such is the migratory character of this people that it is impossible to keep track of them." MEC *neomejicano* converts showed up throughout the Southwest. The new economy in New Mexico and throughout the Southwest made it impossible for people who had lived off the land, some for over two centuries, to survive in the area any longer. Mexican American Protestants apparently fared no better than Catholics in this respect.[15]

Distinctives of Mexican American Protestantism in New Mexico and Colorado

There were many similarities between Mexican American Protestants throughout the Southwest. But there were also several key differences between the northern New Mexico/southern Colorado region and other parts of the Southwest. These were largely due to the unique history and subsequent development of northern New Mexico/southern Colorado. This region had been isolated from central Mexico during Spanish rule. As a part of Mexico from 1821 to 1846, its ties to the central government were weak, and some *neomejicanos* thought the area should join the United States. The U.S. takeover further weakened ties to Mexico and isolated *neomejicanos* from other Mexican Americans in the Southwest. Other parts of the Southwest, such as Texas, southern Arizona, and southern California, had a much closer relationship to Mexico. During the nineteenth century people moving north and south kept these ties strong. Northern New Mexico and southern Colorado were not a part of these migratory patterns, so they become more isolated from Mexico and other Mexican Americans in the Southwest.

Mexican American Protestantism likewise reflected this divide between northern New Mexico/southern Colorado and the rest of the Southwest. The churches in northern New Mexico and southern Colorado remained relatively isolated from the Protestant movement in Mexico and from other Mexican American Protestants in the United States. In contrast, most Mexican American Protestant leaders in other parts of the Southwest had strong ties to Mexico or were Mexican immigrants themselves. The isolation did not directly affect Protestant churches in New Mexico and Colorado until the beginning of the twentieth century. Just as Mexican American Protestantism started to grow in most of the Southwest, it began to decline in northern New Mexico and southern Colorado.[16] Several *neomejicano* Protestant leaders migrated to other parts of the Southwest to continue in ministry after the churches in New Mexico began to decline in size.

Relations between Anglo and Mexican American Protestants

Little is written about the relationship between Anglo and Mexican American Protestants in the nineteenth century. Anglo missionaries wrote all the few extant comments related to the issue. The little that is known is probably best summarized in Carolyn Zeleny's description of *neomejicano* Protestants at the beginning of this chapter.

Reports about Protestant work among Mexican Americans during the nineteenth century describe a relationship in which the Anglo missionaries held all the principal leadership positions; Mexican American leaders were always subordinate to them. This inequality stands out most clearly among the PCUSA in New Mexico, who maintained high requirements for ordination that made it almost impossible for *neomejicanos* to obtain that status. Throughout the nineteenth century very few Mexican American Presbyterian ministers were ordained as pastors. Presbyterian records list them as licentiates or evangelists, even though many were responsible for congregations and had years of experience in the ministry (e.g., Mondragón, Romero, and Gallegos). All licentiates had to be under an ordained pastor, who was always Anglo.[17] This did not change until the beginning of the twentieth century, when the number of ordained Mexican American pastors began to grow.

The subordinate status of Mexican American Protestants manifested itself in other ways. Anglos usually controlled the publication of Protestant materials in Spanish, although many of them did not speak or write the language well.[18] Spanish-language congregations were named after Anglo missionaries (Pyle Memorial in Taos) or placed in a subordinate status to English-language congregations. For example, many Mexican American congregations were "Second" Presbyterian Churches, even those started before the English language congregations. The most extreme cases were the Second Presbyterian Church in Las Vegas, which was started before the Anglo congregation, but was still referred to as the second church, and La Jara Second Presbyterian Church, which was not even in the town of La Jara. Decisions about Protestant work in the Southwest were almost completely in the hands of Anglos. When churches were dissolved it was assumed that Mexican Americans would join the congregation that Anglos decided would be best for them. For example, Presbyterian Church in Anaheim was dissolved in 1882 and its members added to the Anglo congregation.[19] The congregation at Socorro, New Mexico, was started by the Baptists, became Methodist at the recommendation of a former Baptist missionary, Shaw, and was later made a Presbyterian congregation by missionary decision.[20] Missionaries also decided who could be an evangelist, how they would be trained, who would receive a salary, and how much they would receive.[21]

Latino Responses to Anglo American Dominance

Since missionaries wrote almost all we know about Mexican American Protestantism during the nineteenth century, we have only their version of the tensions between them and Mexican American leaders. But there is enough evidence to demonstrate that there were problems in several denominations. The first record of interpersonal conflict between an Anglo missionary and a Mexican American was that between John Annin and José Ynés Perea. Perea, who was from a wealthy family, financially supported Annin in his efforts in Las Vegas. The relationship became strained on several occasions when Annin attempted to impose his ideas merely because he was an Anglo—even though he was often financially dependent on Perea.[22]

Thomas Harwood, MEC missionary in New Mexico, had problems with several Mexican American pastors. During his early years (1870s), Harwood's memoirs refer to tension with a former Baptist pastor, Blas Chávez, and with Juan García, a licensed MEC pastor. The latter situation was so severe that several *neomejicano* pastors sent a letter to the New York headquarters of the MEC home mission society. Harwood was apparently reprimanded for his attitude and actions toward

García, but he relentlessly defended them in his memoirs.[23] During his latter years as superintendent of the New Mexico Spanish Mission Conference, Harwood attempted to have the Mexican American pastors vote to petition the denominational offices for their acceptance as an Annual Conference. *Neomejicano* pastors voted against the plan during the annual session (in which the MEC bishop was present) for reasons not completely clear. Harwood made no others effort of this type.[24]

The most overt tensions occurred between Anglo and Mexican American Baptists in Texas. Manuel Treviño, a former MECS pastor, was ordained by the BGC and began working in San Antonio in 1888. Several congregations were started under his leadership. In 1891 the Baptist General Convention named C. D. Daniel, a former missionary in Latin America, to work in Texas. Daniel was assigned to oversee the work and Treviño became an itinerant evangelist. This seemed to work for a while, but Treviño and another Mexican American pastor resigned within a year. They later returned to the work, but apparently the tensions remained. Records of the period refer to a problem between Daniel and Treviño but do not clarify the reasons for Treviño's resignation. According to the Baptist historian Joshua Grijalva, the problem was doctrinal: Daniel supposedly exposed the fact that Treviño was a Campbellite, believing that baptism was necessary for salvation.[25]

This explanation seems incomplete, at best. Baptist leaders ordained Treviño and the BGC highly praised him both before and after his resignation. This suggests that the issue was not primarily doctrinal. Treviño was reported to have been as successful (or more successful) than Daniel in starting new churches. When Treviño resigned, he also had the support of other *tejano* leaders. Treviño disappeared from Baptist records after 1894 with no explanation of his departure. Daniel became a key leader in Spanish language Baptist work in Texas during the first part of the twentieth century.

The Bible in Mexican American Protestant Folklore[26]

The Bible played a very important part in nineteenth-century Mexican American Protestant life. The general view was that any person who sincerely read the Bible would choose to become a Protestant. Several of the early Protestant missionaries were colporteurs, selling and donating Spanish-language Bibles. Protestant missionaries and evangelists would often go house to house reading the Bible to anyone who would listen to them. Protestants often told stories about the impact that reading the Bible had on people. In New Mexico and Colorado, Protestants began telling stories about specific Bibles and their impact. Several of "these unique Bibles . . . entered into Protestant Hispanic folklore . . . named for the families [or communities] that became Protestant because of them."[27] The stories that developed around several of these Spanish Bibles served as testimonies to strengthen the faithful, particularly in New Mexico and Colorado. They became part of the story around which Mexican American Protestants began to define their identity.

The Chimayó Bible

The Chimayó Bible is named for the community of Chimayó, New Mexico. Zoe Ellsworth, a Presbyterian teacher working in Chimayó, recorded this story: Don Agapito Ortega, an elderly woodcutter and handyman, showed Ellsworth an old Bible and told her its story. Agapito's father was a trader before the arrival of the railroad. One day he took a load of chili to Colorado to trade for wheat. He saw a Spanish Bible in a storefront window. He was intrigued by it because the priest in his village had forbidden the people to own one. Ortega inquired about the price, which the shopkeeper set at ten dollars (much too high). Ortega bought it for that price, relinquishing most of what he had earned from his trading. When he returned home he decided to hide the Bible, because he was afraid that someone would take it from him—and because he did not know how to read. He kept the Bible a secret until on his deathbed, when he bequeathed it to his eldest son. The elder son gave it to Agapito. As a grown man, Agapito learned to read and was converted through his Bible reading. He used the Bible throughout his life and, before he died, gave it to Miss Ellsworth.[28]

The Congregational Bible

The *Home Missionary*, a publication of the Congregational Church, records the story of a Bible that did not become famous enough to receive a specific name.[29] According to the article, a missionary distributing Bibles gave one to a Mexican lady during the 1850s. She carefully stored it away in a treasure box and left it there, unread, for almost twenty years. One day a Mexican soldier who had married her niece mentioned something he had read in a New Testament lent to him by a comrade during the Civil War. The aunt informed him that she too had a Bible. He offered to trade it for a Catechism and she accepted. He read the Bible, was converted, and became a preacher of the gospel. At least thirty people had converted under his ministry by the time the article was written. The article states that the missionary who distributed the Bible never saw the fruit of his labor, "but God's word did not return void."

The Gómez Bible

Francis Gilchrist, PCUSA missionary in New Mexico and Colorado, published the story of a Bible purchased by Juan Gómez, a cattle and sheep farmer in what is now southern Colorado. In 1868 he purchased a Bible from a Frenchman for the equivalent of about sixty dollars in cash, animals, and the usage of a pair of oxen. According to Gilchrist, this high cost apparently was not unknown for old Bibles such as this one because they were passed secretly from hand to hand. A Catholic priest often stayed at the Gómez home when he visited the area. During one of these stays he found the Bible and read it extensively. Instead of castigating Gómez, the priest encouraged him to *"Mídase usted por esa vara y guíese por ella, Señor Gómez* [Measure yourself with that yardstick and be guided by it, Mr. Gómez]."

After this encouragement, the Gómez family started a Bible study. Gómez, members of his family, and several friends became a part of this group. When Alexander Darley visited the area in the late 1870s, he met with the Bible study group and eventually organized them into a Presbyterian church. The group was very influential throughout the rest of the nineteenth century, and members of the group helped start other congregations in southern Colorado. At least three of Juan Gómez's grandchildren assumed important leadership roles among Spanish-speaking Presbyterians in southern Colorado and New Mexico: Manuel D. J. Sánchez, an early graduate of the College of the Southwest, served as a pastor throughout the Southwest for many years. His brother Gabriel was also an ordained Presbyterian minister. Marcelina, their sister, married Refugio Jaramillo, an important Mexican American Presbyterian leader during the late nineteenth and early twentieth century. One of Manuel's daughters, Ema, married Amadeo Maés, a Presbyterian pastor who worked in Colorado, New Mexico, and California.[30] The Bible was handed down from generation to generation. It has been put on display several times during the twentieth century, including a presentation at the American Bible Society in New York.[31]

The Madrid Bible

Descendants of Albino Madrid relate that the Madrid Bible was apparently found on the side of a road in the early 1880s. The person who found it did not know its value and traded it to Albino Madrid for a Spanish speller and primer. Madrid began to study it carefully and soon understood it enough to raise questions about traditional Catholicism. On a trip to Las Vegas, New Mexico, Madrid ran into a group of Protestants, who explained more of the Bible to him and gave him tracts. Enthused by this experience, Madrid began inviting people for Bible study sessions in his home. After studying the Bible and tracts given to them by Gabino Rendón, Madrid's group became convinced that Catholicism was in error. Madrid and several others (including his nephew Manuel Madrid, who later became a PCUSA missionary) were converted to Protestantism. The group joined the Presbyterian Church in Las Vegas, and Presbyterians later started a mission in Madrid's home.[32] Several of Madrid's descendants continued in the Presbyterian Church into the twentieth century.[33]

The Ocaté Bible

Dora Ortiz Vásquez, a *neomejicano* Presbyterian, recounted the story of the Ocaté Bible. Amadeo Maés was the son of one of Padre Martínez's followers during the 1850s. Maés inherited a Bible from his father, but his enemies labeled him a heretic and burned both the Bible and his house. But Maés vowed to find another Bible to replace the one he had lost. One day, after helping put out a forest fire, Maés began talking with some of the other firefighters of things that seemed strange to most of them. They asked how he knew about such things. When he told them he had learned them from the Bible, the men told Maés that there was a man in the town of Mora who owned one. Maés found the man and bought the Bible from him for two tailored suits (Maés was a tailor), two calves, a few sheep, farm produce, and twenty-five pesos. His neighbors helped him pay for the Bible so it became common property among them.

The Bible could not be read openly, so Maés created a small meeting place in his cellar. Almost every night several neighbors would get together to read the Bible and memorize parts of it.

When James Roberts visited the area, "he found a group of more than twenty people ready to join a church" and in 1875 he organized the Ocaté group into a church.[34]

The Peralta Bible

This is the only Bible that became a part of *neomejicano* MEC folklore. According to Thomas Harwood, E. J. Nicholson, the first MEC missionary in New Mexico, left this Bible with Ambrosio Gonzales of Peralta in the early 1850s. Gonzales began to read it, particularly Genesis and the book of John. He was convicted by what he had heard from Nicholson and read in the Bible. He became a Protestant and was named leader of a Sunday school that was organized in his home by Dalas Lore in 1855. Under Gonzales's leadership, the Peralta congregation survived and grew after all the Protestant missionaries left the area during the Civil War.[35]

The Sánchez Bible

Francis Gilchrist, in 1857, also published the story of the Sánchez Bible. Pedro Sánchez purchased it for a fat ox worth about twenty-five dollars. Sánchez died without ever meeting a Protestant missionary, but his brothers-in-law, Pablo and Pedro Ortega, and their families learned about the gospel by reading this Bible. PCUSA missionary James Roberts found the Ortegas in 1878. Soon afterward a Presbyterian church was formed in Cenicero, the first among the Spanish-speaking communities of Colorado. Presbyterians later organized two daughter churches from this original congregation.[36]

1900 Census of Mexican American Protestants[37]

At the beginning of the twentieth century most Mexican American Protestants were Methodists and the largest concentration of

Mexican American Protestants was in northern New Mexico/ southern Colorado. If one adds the membership of the MEC and the MECS, over half of all Mexican American Protestants were Methodists. The PCUSA was the third largest denomination with 26.3 percent of the membership and when combined with the PCUS, Presbyterians constituted 35.6 percent of Mexican American Protestants. Southern Baptists made up 6.5 percent of the total, and Congregationalists and Disciples of Christ were only nominally represented (Graph 3). There was slow but steady growth in the number of Mexican American Protestants throughout the nineteenth century, with the MEC growing the most.

Review by State/Territory

From 1887 to 1900, the largest concentration of Mexican American Protestants lived in the Territory of New Mexico (which also had the largest Mexican American population). Protestant

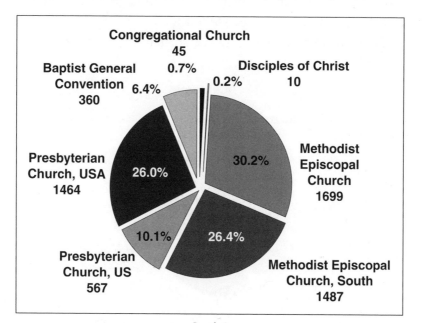

Graph 3
Mexican American Protestants by Denominations, 1900
Southwestern United States

work among Mexican Americans in Texas grew more rapidly than in New Mexico from 1894, and by 1900 there were almost as many Mexican American Protestants in Texas as in New Mexico. The overwhelming majority (87.9 percent) of all Mexican American Protestants lived in New Mexico and Texas. Colorado accounted for 8.3 percent of Mexican American Protestant church members. California and Arizona together had less than 4 percent of the total (Graph 4).

Mexican American Protestant membership growth was most consistent in New Mexico. It was not rapid, but it was steady throughout the nineteenth century.[38] Texas, on the other hand, went through spurts. From 1870 to 1880 the *tejano* Protestant population boomed, and by 1880 there were twice as many Spanish-speaking Protestants in Texas as in New Mexico. But there was little growth during the 1880s in Texas and by 1887 there were, once again, more Mexican American Protestants in New Mexico. From 1888 to 1895 growth was roughly parallel in both areas. After 1895 it leveled off in New Mexico while growth continued in Texas, so that by the beginning of

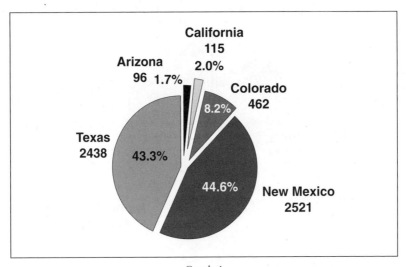

Graph 4
Mexican American Protestants by States, 1900
Southwestern United States

the twentieth century there were more Mexican American Protestants in Texas than in New Mexico. Growth in Arizona, California, and Colorado was very slow throughout most of the nineteenth century. From 1895 to 1900 Arizona suffered a major membership loss, and Colorado began to experience a period of steady growth. California's membership growth remained slow until the beginning of the twentieth century.

An overview of the number of churches established during the nineteenth century demonstrates a slightly different pattern. From 1870 through 1881 about half of all Mexican American congregations were located in Texas. Then MEC growth tipped the balance toward New Mexico. From 1884 to 1900 over 50 percent of all Mexican American congregations in the Southwest were located in New Mexico. By 1900 there were 150 Mexican American Protestant congregations in the Southwest with most located in Northern New Mexico or in Central Texas (Map 7).[39]

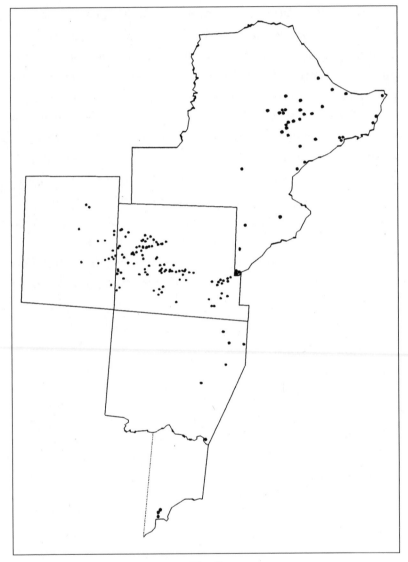

Map 7
Geographic Distribution of Mexican American Protestant
Churches and Preaching Points, 1900, Southwestern United States

Conclusion

BEGINNINGS OF A NEW SUBCULTURE

AS THE NINETEENTH CENTURY CAME TO A CLOSE, MOST MEXICAN Americans occupied the fringes of U.S. society. The vast majority lived in isolated areas, such as south Texas and northern New Mexico, with a growing number in urban barrios. They inhabited their own subculture on the lower rungs of the new economic order. Mexican American Protestants were even more isolated. Their religious commitment isolated them from their own people. Many had believed that by becoming Protestants they would be able to enter Anglo American society and partake of the "American" ideal. But for the vast majority, conversion to Protestantism did not open doors within the larger U.S. society. Most U.S. Protestants did not want Mexican Americans to continue as Catholics, but neither were they willing to accept them as equals when they became Protestants.

Most Mexican American Protestant congregations were small, but they had many highly committed members. Many willingly made great sacrifices in identifying with their new faith. A shared experience of radical conversion, religious persecution, and social isolation gave these people a common identity. But that identity was difficult to define and maintain. Protestantism was so closely affiliated with Anglo American culture that it was difficult for Mexican Americans to think of becoming Protestants without cutting their ties to their cultural heritage. Nonetheless, Mexican American Protestants in the United States were becoming a new subculture in the Borderlands of the Southwest.

The migrating patterns created by the new socio-economic order created a migrating faith among Mexican American Protestants. On the one hand, migration from Mexico brought Mexican Protestants into the existing communities of the Southwest. But on the other hand, Mexican American migrants also took their faith with them. New congregations throughout the Southwest were started when Mexican American Protestants established themselves in new areas.

Pastors and leaders also migrated with the people. Throughout the first half of the twentieth century, people who had been formed in these nineteenth-century congregations pastored Mexican American Protestant churches in the Southwest. Another type of migration happened after the beginning of the Pentecostal movement. Many of the early Mexican American pastors in Pentecostal churches were former Methodist or Presbyterian pastors that converted to Pentecostalism. And they continued migrating with their people who often also became Pentecostals.

These converts were joined by new waves of immigrants from Mexico. The growing number of converts meant that the number and size of churches continued to grow. But their growing size did not fundamentally change the challenge of life and identity in the Southwest. Mexican Americans and Mexican immigrants had to deal with how to adapt to American culture. And Protestantism continued to offer an individualistic, yet unsure, bridge toward the future for many. Mexican American Protestantism became a part of the Borderlands religious identity. Mexican Americans converted to Protestantism, but did not necessarily fully Americanize. They began a process that continues to this day. Luis León's description of Chicano Protestants at the end of the twentieth century has its roots in these converts: "Chicano *evangélicos* appropriate Protestantism, inflect it and mirror it back, changing the Protestant symbolic language of North America, figuring it with distinctively Mexican-American grammars."[1]

Protestant missionaries took outside structures, Protestant churches and schools, into the Mexican American community. The converts were never able to take control of the schools, but they were given some voice over the churches, at least at the local level. The missionaries also brought religious symbols and rituals with them that were foreign to Mexican Americans.[2] The converts began to reinterpret two important Protestant symbols—the Bible of the Protestant Reformation, and the radical religious conversion of Pietist renewal—and make them part of their own ethno-religious identity. In this sense they were similar to Protestant converts in Latin America. But because of the added pressure of cultural assimilation, Mexican American Protestants struggled, and continue to struggle, with the maintenance of that identity from generation to generation. The isolated communities of south Texas or northern New Mexico were able to maintain some identity stability. But the migrating Mexican American Protestants in the Borderlands continue to change and adapt as did those of the late nineteenth century.

Today the Mexican American Protestants of the nineteenth-century southwestern United States have been largely forgotten. Although they were the pioneers of Latino Protestantism, both Protestant denominations and Latino historians largely overlook their role. This oversight is due to several factors. First, their tenuous existence among Anglo American Protestants and predominantly Catholic Mexican Americans makes it difficult to define their place in nineteenth-century American religious history. They were Protestants, but they represented such a minuscule part of American Protestantism that very little has been written about them from that perspective. They were also Mexican Americans, but they were not Catholics. Therefore, studies of nineteenth-century Mexican Americans have either ignored

them or referred to them only briefly, focusing on the importance of Catholicism in defining nineteenth-century Mexican
American religious experience.[3]

Second, the Mexican American Protestant churches of New
Mexico and southern Colorado (where almost half of all Mexican American Protestants lived in 1900) began to decline during the first years of the twentieth century. Most of the congregations disappeared or were absorbed into English-language
churches. Very few of the original churches have remained, and
most of those still in existence are in very isolated communities,
far from the mainstream of Latino Protestantism. The Mexican
American Protestants who migrated to other areas from this region joined with migrants from other areas and their *neomejicano* regional identity tended to dissipate in the midst of people
from other parts of the Southwest and Mexico.

A third factor relates to the constant migratory patterns of
Latinos, and Latino Protestants in particular. Protestant work
among the Spanish-speaking population began in earnest when
large numbers of immigrants began arriving from Mexico during the Mexican Revolution (1910–1920). Each wave of immigrants from Latin America has marked a new chapter in Protestant work among Latinos. The twin forces of cultural
assimilation and new immigration have created a discontinuity
of narratives between generations of Latino Protestants.

José Ynés Perea, the first Mexican American ordained as a
PCUSA pastor, is probably a fitting representative of the nineteenth-century Mexican American Protestant community. He
followed a lonely path in his Protestant commitment—one that
included isolation and cultural assimilation. Perea sacrificed
family and fortune to follow Jesus Christ, within a Protestant
framework, and to serve as a Protestant pastor for the rest of his
life. He was a part of a generation of pioneers who paid dearly
for their conversion. Perea was convinced that his people needed
to be converted to Protestantism if they were to know true faith

in Christ, but his energetic commitment and effort never produced the results for which he longed. Few people responded to his preaching, and the congregations he established did not outlive him. Yet he never wavered in his commitment to Protestantism; it was there that he had found new life in Jesus Christ and the strength to walk this lonely path.

José Inés Perea

Perea's story is unknown to most Latino Protestants today. Yet his story became an important part of the religious narrative that undergirded the identity of early twentieth-century Mexican American Protestants in the Southwest. And by the time his story was lost in Protestant folklore, it had been replaced by many other stories similar to his. New converts heard the stories of new "Pereas" who sacrificed all to follow Jesus.

Latino Protestantism is a religious manifestation of the Borderlands. It began in the Southwest and continues to attract new generations of Latinos in the region. It lives and thrives at the crossroads between Catholicism and Protestantism, premodernity, modernity and post-modernity and the encounter between first and developing worlds in the midst of a globalized economy. People continue to be attracted to the "light" of Latino Protestantism as they seek purpose and meaning to life in the Borderlands.

Appendix: Mexican American Protestant Church Members by Denomination and State, 1870–1900

	1870	1871	1872	1873	1874	1875	1876	1877	1878	1879	1880	1881	1882	1883	1884	1885	1886	1887	1888	1889	1890	1891	1892	1893	1894	1895	1896	1897	1898	1899	1900
Baptist General Convention																			9	51	75	80	112	271	234	236	200	240	280	320	360
Texas																			9	51	75	80	112	271	234	236	200	240	280	320	360
Congregationalist Church																						11	15	19	23	27	31	35	38	42	45
New Mexico																						11	15	19	23	27	31	35	38	42	45
Disciples of Christ																														8	10
Texas																														8	10
Methodist Episcopal Church	15	20	60	95	134	166	245	432	565	651	709	718	735	762	903	815	936	954	887	931	1020	1118	1207	1447	1556	1654	1679	1725	1820	1731	1699
Arizona																						12	21	76	71	105	157	147	140	150	59
California																															
Colorado																						31	24	37	87	89	11	47	46	46	52
New Mexico	15	20	60	95	134	166	245	432	565	651	709	718	735	762	903	815	936	954	887	931	1020	1075	1162	1238	1312	1430	1483	1489	1579	1488	1537
Texas																								96	86	30	28	42	55	47	51
Methodist Episcopal Church, South							75	106	141	170	195	243	270	293	312	408	550	668	654	822	945	1092	1166	1275	1383	1425	1454	1519	1531	1468	1487
Arizona																							9	25	35	40	41	35	27	33	37
Presbyterian Church, US (South)								10	12	15	17	21	23	30	33	35	31	37	64	65	73	95	111	150	188	228	321	345	369	425	567
Texas (West Texas Presbytery)								10	12	15	17	21	23	30	33	35	31	37	25	25	32	52	67	108	143	182	273	300	320	376	517
Brownsville, Texas (Tamaulipas Presbytery)																			39	40	41	43	44	42	45	46	48	45	49	49	50
Presbyterian Church, USA (North)	12	21	14	13	25	26	34	72	95	129	186	231	306	427	444	448	406	464	579	676	802	897	889	1096	1223	1323	1326	1406	1368	1417	1464
Arizona																						26	20	59	80	92	93	124	61		
California																				15	42	76	75	84	87	92	93	82	89	106	115
Colorado																					101	101	99	184	216	254	296	336	346	387	410
New Mexico											132	162	184	214	251	279	259	312	442	516	635	694	695	769	840	885	844	864	872	924	939
TOTALS	27	52	72	120	180	240	354	620	813	965	1107	1213	1334	1512	1692	1706	1923	2123	2193	2545	2915	3293	3500	4258	4607	4893	5011	5270	5406	5411	5632
TOTALS BY STATE																															
Arizona	12	21	14	13	25	26	34															38	50	160	186	237	291	306	228	183	96
California																				15	42	76	75	84	87	92	93	82	89	106	115
Colorado																					101	132	123	221	303	343	307	383	392	433	462
New Mexico	15	20	60	95	134	166	245	432	565	651	841	880	919	976	1154	1094	1195	1266	1329	1447	1655	1780	1872	2026	2175	2342	2358	2388	2489	2454	2521
Texas							75	116	153	185	212	264	293	323	345	443	581	705	727	938	1093	1267	1380	1767	1856	1879	1962	2111	2208	2235	2438

NOTATIONS

1. Numbers in italics are estimates, used when no statistical data was reported.

2. The MEC, MECS, PCUSA, and PCUS all kept detailed membership reports for their churches. The only significant exception is the MECS in Texas for 1900. No membership totals were reported that year. Totals for 1900 are estimated from 1899 and 1901 totals.

3. Baptist General Convention records in Texas are sketchy and incomplete for the nineteenth century. There are no statistical reports from 1894–1900. The estimated totals for those years are based on earlier totals and on statistical reports after 1900.

4. Congregational Church records for New Mexico are not clear. The estimates are based on the membership list of *neomejicano* members listed as a part of Albuquerque Congregational Church in 1891, missionary reports, and membership totals after 1900.

5. There are no membership totals for the Disciples of Christ congregation in San Antonio. The estimate is based on one report in 1899 that states that several Mexicans were baptized and a 1908 report that the congregation in San Antonio was reorganized with 14 members (see *Survey of Service Organizations*, pp. 121–22).

6. The PCUS congregation in Brownsville was never a part of the West Texas Presbytery during the nineteenth century. It was a part of the Tamaulipas (Mexico) Presbytery well into the twentieth century. No statistical records were found for the nineteenth or first part of the twentieth century. Membership estimates are based on patterns of other PCUS churches in the state.

7. MECS records do not make it clear where one of the congregations (La Luz) was located. In most statistical records it is listed in Texas. But the 1899 records state that it was in New Mexico. For statistical purposes its membership totals are recorded as being a part of Texas.

Notes

INTRODUCTION

1. Gastón Espinosa, Virgilio Elizondo and Jesse Miranda, *Hispanic Churches in American Public Life* (Notre Dame, Ind.: Institute for Latino Studies, 2003), 12–14.

2. See *The Legacy of Conquest: The Unbroken Past of the American West* (W.W. Norton, 1987) by Patricia Nelson Limerick for an excellent introduction to the broader scope and implications of the conquest of the Southwest to this day.

CHAPTER 1

1. According to Ellsworth, "no war waged by the United States, previously or subsequently, have the [Protestant] clergy protested more stoutly," "American Churches and the Mexican War," *American Historical Review* 45, no. 2 (1940): 326. The only other war that has generated so much opposition in the United States has been the Vietnam Conflict.

2. Frederick Merk (*Manifest Destiny and Mission in American History*, Vintage Books, 1963) describes this debate as two competing visions of the United States, the imperialism and continentalism of Manifest Destiny and the ideal of Mission, the view that the United States would serve as an example of freedom to the world.

3. Anonymous, "Memorial Against the War" (drafted and signed by Unitarian pastors and laymen; addressed to the Senate and the House of Representatives) *Christian Register* 25, no. 46 (1847): 182.

4. Statement by the Worchester Baptist Association, 1846, 7.

5. Congregational Ministries and Church in Vermont, Extracts from the Minutes of the General Convention Session, 1847, 7.

6. Presbyterian Church, United States of America, Minutes of the General Assembly, 1846, 216–17.

7. See, for example, Samuel Johnson, "A Fast Day Sermon," *Christian Register* 26, no. 21 (1847): 81; John H. Morison, "The War," *Christian Register* 26, no. 16 (1847): 62; A. P. Peabody, "Ringing Bells for Victories in War," *Christian Register* 26, no. 23 (1847): 89; Dr. Putnam, "Allegiance to Government," *Christian Register* 26, no. 19 (1847): 74; William P. Tilden, "War," *Christian Register* 26, no. 4 (1847): 13; and President Woods, "President Woods on Peace," *Christian Register* 26, no. 2 (1847): 1.

8. Presbyterian Church, United States of America (Minutes of the General Assembly 1846), 222.

9. Theodore Parker, "The Mexican War," *Massachusetts Quarterly Review*, December 1847, 52; Thomas E. Thomas, "Covenant Breaking, and its Consequences or the Present Posture of Our National Affairs, in Connection with the Mexican War," Two Discourses preached in Hamilton, Ohio, July 4 and 11 (Rossville, Ohio: J. M. Christy, Printer, 1847), 36.

10. Samuel Harris, "The Mexican War," A Sermon delivered on the Annual Thanksgiving at Conway, Mass., November 26, 1846 (Greenfield, Mass.: Merriam and Mirick, Printers, 1847), 21.

11. Abiel Abbot Livermore, *The War with Mexico Revisited* (Boston: The American Peace Society, 1850), 31.

12. John Morison, "Extension of Slavery," *Christian Register* 26, no. 5 (1847): 18.

13. Albert Barnes, "Home Missions," A Sermon in Behalf of the American Home Missionary Society (New York: William Osborn, for the American Home Missionary Society, 1849), 9.

14. Harris, "Mexican War," 14, 15.

15. Ibid., 18–19.

16. Thomas, "Covenant Breaking," 72.

17. Anonymous-Pax, "The Mexican War; A New Plan," *Christian Register* 26, no. 3 (1847): 10.

18. Burdett Hart, "Better Things than War," A Discourse delivered at the Congregational Church in Faith Haven on the Annual Thanksgiving of 1847 (New Haven: Peck and Stafford, Printers, 1847), 14. Another writer attacked a statement by the Evangelical Alliance that contended that Americans should exult because the soldiers going into Mexico were, in a sense, missionaries to the Catholic population of that country; Anonymous-Peter the Hermit, "Every Soldier a Missionary," *Christian Register* 26, no. 50 (1847): 198.

19. Livermore, *War with Mexico Revisited*, 212.

20. This perspective was based on the argument used by President James Polk in calling for war against Mexico. President Polk had ordered American soldiers to go all the way to the Rio Grande. Mexico and the United States had a territorial dispute over the land between the Nueces and Rio Grande rivers. So Mexico interpreted this action as an invasion and attacked the soldiers, killing a couple of them. President Polk used this event to ask Congress for a declaration of war against Mexico, claiming that American soldiers had been killed on American soil. So, since Mexico had "attacked first," the U.S. invasion of Mexico was justified as an act of self-defense.

21. Thomas Smyth, "The Relations of Christianity to War: And the Portraiture of a Christian Soldier," A Discourse delivered on occasion of the First Commencement of the Citadel Academy (Charleston, S.C.: B. Jenkins, 1847), 5.

22. Anonymous, review of "Relations of Christianity to War: And the Portraiture of a Christian Soldier" by Rev. Thomas Smyth, *Southern Presbyterian Review* 1, no. 1 (1847): 171.

23. Smyth, "Relations of Christianity to War," 30.

24. Methodist Episcopal Church, South (Minutes of the Annual Conference, 1851), 12.

25. Peabody, "Ringing Bells for Victories," 89.

26. John R. Bodo, *The Protestant Clergy and Public Issues, 1812–1848* (Princeton, N.J.: Princeton University Press, 1954), 225.

27. Josiah Strong, *Our Country; Its Possible Future and Its Present Crisis* (New York: The Baker and Taylor Co., 1858), 174.

28. Frederick Merk´s distinction between Manifest Destiny and Mission (*Manifest Destiny and Mission in American History,* New York: Vintage Books, 1966) is difficult to draw in relationship to the war with Mexico. Though some Protestant leaders seem to make a distinction, the difference between Manifest Destiny and Mission was mostly one of degree and not of substance. Most were convinced that the Southwest legitimately belonged to Americans, even though they might think it was wrong to take the land by force.

29. Livermore, *War with Mexico Revisited,* 210.

30. Parker, "The Mexican War," 51.

31. Erskine Mason, "An Evangelical Ministry, the Security of a Nation," A Sermon preached on behalf of the American Home Missionary Society, January 8, 1848 (New York: William Osborn, 1848), 6.

32. Report presented by the Executive Committee, American Home Missionary Society, 1847, 110.

33. "Present Relative Position." A Report presented to the American Home Missionary Society (New York: American Home Missionary Society, 1849), 48.

34. Hollis Read, *The Hand of God in History, or, Divine Providence Historically Illustrated in the Extension and Establishment of Christianity* (Hartford: H.E. Robins and Company, 1858), 173.

35. Strong, *Our Country,* 173.

36. J. J. Miter, Address to the Home Missionary Society in the 20th Report of the American Home Missionary Society (New York: William Osborn, 1846), 119.

37. Reports presented by the Executive Committee, American Home Missionary Society (New York: American Home Missionary Society, 1846), 101.

38. Morison, "Extension of Slavery," 18.

39. Richard Storrs, *Discourse in Behalf of the American Home Missionary Society* (New York: American Home Missionary Society, 1855), 12.

40. Executive Committee, American Home Missionary Society 1846, 101.

41. Miter, Address to the Home Missionary Society (1846), 116.

42. Hart, "Better Things than War."

43. Livermore, *War with Mexico Revisited,* 212.

44. Ibid., 224. It is interesting to note the assumption that Mexico would have been open to selling its national territory to the United States.

45. Read, *Hand of God in History,* 177.

46. Methodist Episcopal Church, South 1851, 12.

47. Read, *Hand of God in History,* 35–36.

48. Livermore, *War with Mexico Revisited,* 211.

49. Read, *Hand of God in History,* 135, 137, 177.

50. J. N. Granger, "Relative Claims of the Foreign and the Home Fields," *The Baptist Missionary Magazine* 28, no. 10 (1848): 386–87.

51. Barnes, "Home Missions," 17.

52. Read, *Hand of God in History,* 43.

53. Livermore, *War with Mexico Revisited,* 177.

54. W. W. H. Davis, *El Gringo or New Mexico and her People* (Santa Fe: Rydal Press, 1938), 85.

55. William Jay, *A Review of the Causes and Consequences of the Mexican War* (Boston: Benjamin B. Mussey and Company, 1849), 270.

56. H. Forrester, Report from New Mexico and Arizona to the Domestic Committee of the Board of Missions of the Protestant Episcopal Church in the United States of America, 1877, 4.

57. *Baptist Almanac* (Philadelphia: American Baptist Publication Society, 1851), 19.

58. Anonymous, "Occupation of Mexico," *United States Magazine and Democratic Review* 21, no.113 (1847): 388.

59. William W. Phillips, An address, delivered at Peekskill, New York, October 21, 1846 before the Synod of New York by their appointment, and published at their request (Board of Foreign Missions of the Presbyterian Church, 1846), 5.

60. Anonymous, "Occupation of Mexico," 388.

61. Read, *Hand of God in History,* 176.

CHAPTER 2

1. According to Mark Banker (*Presbyterian Missions and Cultural Interaction in the Far Southwest 1850–1950,* University of Illinois Press, 1993, p. 9) Presbyterians lumped Indians, New Mexicans, and Mormons under the category "exceptional populations of the Southwest" as a way of defining the difference between themselves and the peoples they found in the Southwest.

2. Latinos themselves would also use the concept of being "strangers in their own land" as they described their experience in the Southwest after the

American conquest: John Chávez, *The Lost Land: The Chicano Image of the Southwest* (Albuquerque: University of New Mexico Press, 1984), 43.

3. William Stuart Red, *A History of the Presbyterian Church in Texas* (Austin: The Steck Company, 1936), 25–26.

4. Thomas Harwood, *History of the New Mexico Spanish and English Missions of the Methodist Episcopal Church from 1850–1910*, 2 vols. (Albuquerque: El Abogado Press, 1908), 171, 177.

5. Methodist Episcopal Church, New Mexico Mission Conference, Minutes of the Annual Conference, 1883, 13.

6. Presbyterian Church, United States of America, Board of Home Missions, Annual Report to the General Assembly, 1879, 5–10.

7. Presbyterian Church, United States of America, Board of Home Missions, 1877, 9–10.

8. David H. Moore, "To the Life of Mrs. Emily Jane Harwood," in *Life of Mrs. Emily J. Harwood*, by Harriet Kellogg (Albuquerque: El Abogado Press, 1903), i; T. Harwood, *History of New Mexico . . . Missions*, 1:242; Charles B. Sumner, "New Mexico and Arizona," *The Home Missionary* 58, no. 3 (1885): 111.

9. See Mark Banker, *Presbyterian Missions and Cultural Interaction in the Far Southwest, 1850–1950* (Urbana: University of Illinois Press, 1993) for a description of the Presbyterian perspective on the issue.

10. John C. Calhoun, "The Government of a White Race," in the *Congressional Globe*, 30th Congress, First Session (1848), 98–99.

11. Mario T. García, "The Californios of San Diego and the Politics of Accommodation, 1846–1860," *Aztlán* 6, no. 1 (1975): 76–77.

12. Abiel Abbot Livermore, *The War with Mexico Revisited* (Boston: The American Peace Society, 1850), 177.

13. Walter S. Scott, "The Mexicans in Texas," in *At Our Door: A Study of Home Missions with Special Reference to the South and West*, by Samuel L. Morris (New York: Fleming H. Revell, 1904), 133.

14. *Home Mission Monthly*, September 1887, 246.

15. Baptist General Convention, Texas (Proceedings of the Annual Sessions, 1895), 27.

16. Moore, "Life of Mrs. Emily Jane Harwood," i.

17. Emily Harwood, "Field and Work of the New Mexico Spanish Methodist Episcopal Mission," reprinted from "Gospel in All Lands" (1901), in *Life of Mrs. Emily J. Harwood*, by Harriet Kellogg (Albuquerque: El Abogado Press, 1903), 341.

18. *Home Mission Monthly*, November 1892, 13.

19. *Home Mission Monthly*, August 1894, 229.

20. Horacio Ladd, "University of New Mexico, Santa Fé, N.M." December 20, 1881, document in the Horacio Oliver Ladd File, University Library, University of New Mexico, Albuquerque.

21. *Home Mission Monthly,* September 1887, 245–46.

22. Matilda A. Allison, "Mission Work in New Mexico," *Home Mission Monthly,* September 1887, 249.

23. Walter S. Scott, "Popular Meeting for Home Missions," *Trans-Mississippi Presbyterian,* May 26, 1898, 8; Scott, "Mexicans in Texas," 133.

24. T. Harwood, *History of New Mexico . . . Missions,* 1:210.

25. Allison, "Mission Work in New Mexico," 250.

26. Alice Hyson, "A Visit to One of Our Mission Schools," *Home Mission Monthly,* November 1893, 9.

27. Emily Harwood, "The Mexicans of our Country" (1899), in *Life of Mrs. Emily J. Harwood,* by Harriet Kellogg (Albuquerque: El Abogado Press, 1903), 349.

28. Joseph B. Clark, *Leavening the Nation: The Story of American Home Missions* (New York: Baker and Taylor, 1903), 247.

29. Melinda Rankin, *Twenty Years Among the Mexicans: A Narrative of Missionary Labor* (St. Louis: Christian Publishing Company, 1875), 40–41.

30. Alexander Darley, "Mexican," *Rocky Mountain Presbyterian* 11, no. 19 (October 1880): 153.

31. E. Lyman Hood, "New Mexico and Arizona [II]," *The Home Missionary* 62, no. 12 (April 1890): 524.

32. *The Field Is the World* (organ reviewing the mission work of the Presbyterian Church in the United States of America), November 1880, 133; A Mexican Home Missionary, "From New Mexico, " *The Home Missionary* 59, no. 5 (September 1886), 190; E. Lyman Hood, "New Mexico and Arizona [I]," *The Home Missionary* 62, no. 11 (March 1890): 482.

33. T. Harwood, *History of New Mexico . . . Missions,* 1:20.

34. William Bricen Miller, "Texas Mexican Baptist History, or A History of Baptist Work Among Mexicans in Texas" (Ph.D. diss., Southwestern Baptist Theological Seminary, Fort Worth, Texas, 1931), 12.

35. Mary E. Teats, Introductory Note by the National Evangelist of the Women's Christian Temperance Union in *Life of Mrs. Emily J. Harwood,* by Harriet Kellogg (Albuquerque: El Abogado Press, 1903), iii–iv.

36. Hood, "New Mexico and Arizona [II]," 523.

37. Charles L. Thompson, *The Soul of America: The Contribution of Presbyterian Home Missions* (New York: Fleming H. Revell, 1919), 210–11.

38. B. F. Fuller, *History of Texas Baptists* (Louisville, Ky.: Baptist Book Concern, 1900), 295.

39. *The Field Is the World,* November 1880, 133–34.

40. T. Harwood, *History of New Mexico . . . Missions,* 1:19.

41. Ibid., 1:215, 251.

42. Thompson, *The Soul of America,* 211.

43. T. Harwood, *History of New Mexico . . . Missions,* 1:19.

44. Ibid., 1:206.

45. H. Kendall and Cyrus Dickson, "Appeal to Christian Women," *Rocky Mountain Presbyterian* 11, no. 12 (December 1880): 188.

46. T. Harwood, *History of New Mexico . . . Missions,* 1:213.

47. Kendall and Dickson, "Appeal to Christian Women," 188; Baptist General Convention, Texas, 1889, 18.

48. Quote from Emily Harwood, "Field and Work of the New Mexico Spanish Methodist Episcopal Mission," reprinted from "Gospel in All Lands" (1901), in *Life of Mrs. Emily J. Harwood,* by Harriet Kellogg (Albuquerque: El Abogado Press, 1903), 335. Also, it was the "idolatry" of the Mexicans of San Antonio that "stirred" the first Baptist missionary, Dr. W. D. Powell, to begin work among them in 1887 (Baptist General Convention, Texas, 1888), 8. On Catholicism not a form of Christianity, see Darley, "Mexican," 153.

49. T. Harwood, *History of New Mexico . . . Missions,* 1:178.

50. Ibid., 1:19–20.

51. Rankin, *Twenty Years Among the Mexicans,* 41–42.

52. Baptist General Convention, Blanco Baptist Association, 1886, 3–4.

53. See Susan Yohn, *Contest of Faiths,* for a description of that questioning process among the Presbyterian women missionary teachers in New Mexico.

CHAPTER 3

1. Rankin, *Twenty Years Among the Mexicans,* 51.

2. As quoted by Melinda Rankin, *Twenty Years Among the Mexicans,* 58.

3. In Southern California Latinos remained the majority until twenty years after California became a state (Rodolfo Acuña, *Occupied America: A History of Chicanos,* 3d ed. [New York: HarperCollins, 1988], 112).

4. David H. Moore, "To the Life of Mrs. Emily Jane Harwood," in *Life of Mrs. Emily J. Harwood,* by Harriet Kellogg (Albuquerque: El Abogado Press, 1903), i.

5. E. Lyman Hood, "New Mexico and Arizona [I]," 482.

6. Baptist General Convention, Blanco Baptist Association, 1880, 6.

7. Baptist General Convention, Blanco Baptist Association, 1881, 7.

8. Baptist General Convention, Blanco Baptist Association, 1882.

9. Baptist General Convention, Blanco Baptist Association, 1890.

10. Baptist General Convention, Blanco Baptist Association, 1895, 7.

11. Ibid.

12. Baptist General Convention, Texas, 1889, 18.

13. Baptist General Convention, Texas, 1891, 14.

14. Baptist General Convention, Texas, 1894, 25.

15. Melinda Rankin, *Texas in 1850* (Boston: Damrell and Moore, 1850), 18–20.

16. Walter S. Scott, "The Mexicans in Texas," 131, 134.

17. Matilda Allison, "Letter from Miss Allison," *The Field Is the World*, March 1882, 318.

18. Methodist Episcopal Church, Northern California Conference, Minutes of the Annual Conference, 1881, 51.

19. Methodist Episcopal Church, (Southern) California Conference, Minutes of the Annual Conference, 1882, 22.

20. Douglas R. Brackenridge and Francisco O. García-Treto, *Iglesia Presbiteriana: A History of Presbyterians and Mexican Americans in the Southwest* (San Antonio: Trinity University Press, 1974), 2.

21. Rankin, *Texas in 1850*, 3.

22. Ibid., 195.

23. Ibid., 17, 54, 195.

24. The word *border* is misspelled as "borerd" in the original document.

25. Baptist General Convention, Blanco Baptist Association, 1888, 4.

26. Quoted in Red, *A History of the Presbyterian Church*, 72.

27. Scott, "Mexicans in Texas," 133.

28. These fears were partially based on pronouncements from the Vatican against democracy, freedom of the press, and secular education during the nineteenth century, for example, the *Syllabus of Errors* (1864) and the First Vatican Council (1870).

29. See Ray Allen Billington, *The Protestant Crusade 1800–1860* (1938; repr., Chicago: Quadrangle Books, 1964) for a description of the development of anti-Catholicism among American Protestants during the first part of the nineteenth century.

30. A specific example of the editorial perspective of the magazine is the article "Shall the United States Become Roman Catholic?" *Home Mission Monthly*, April 1891, 130. According to the author, the Roman Catholic Church had a carefully laid out plan to make the United States a Catholic country within a century and had publicly stated its intentions during the Baltimore Council of the American bishops, held during the early 1850s. The working out of this effort could be seen throughout the United States, not only in the Southwest. Protestant missionaries needed to go out to counteract the Catholics' attempts.

31. E. Lyman Hood, "New Mexico and Arizona [II]," *The Home Missionary* 62, no. 12 (April 1890): 525.

32. Paul Horgan (*Lamy of Santa Fe: His Life and Times*, New York: Ferrar, Straus and Giroux, 1975) demonstrates that Lamy was as committed to Americanizing Mexican Catholics as were the Protestants. The Protestant missionaries could not see this because, in their view, Americanization had to be tied to Protestantism.

33. *The Home Missionary,* September 1886, 189.

34. As quoted by Kellogg, *Life of Emily Harwood,* 133.

35. Baptist General Convention, Blanco Baptist Association, 1886, 3.

36. Scott, "Mexicans in Texas," 132–33.

37. Scott, "Mexicans in Texas," 132.

38. Rankin, *Twenty Years Among the Mexicans,* 60.

39. Thomas Bowman, "The Bishop's Letter," Peralta, N.M., District Conference, June 20, 1877, in *History of New Mexico Spanish and English Missions of the Methodist Episcopal Church from 1850–1910,* by Thomas Harwood (Albuquerque: El Abogado Press, 1908), 1:294.

40. Methodist Episcopal Church, (Southern) California, 1882, 25. This
was the common view held by Protestants in general, although there were
fewer than twenty priests throughout the Southwest at the time of the American takeover.

41. This statement is only partially true. The priests discouraged the
people from reading Protestant tracts and Protestant versions of the Bible. But
they also sold Catholic translations of the Bible to the people.

42. *The Home Missionary* 59, no. 7 (November 1886), 280.

43. T. Harwood, *History of New Mexico . . . Missions,* 1:253.

44. *Home Mission Monthly,* September 1887, 243.

45. *Home Mission Monthly,* November 1892, 10.

46. *Home Mission Monthly,* April 1891, 122.

47. *The Home Missionary* 59, no. 5 (September 1886), 189.

48. A. Darley, "Mexican," 153.

49. Harriet Kellogg, *Life of Mrs. Emily J. Harwood,* 48.

50. Robert M. Craig, *Our Mexicans* (New York: The Board of Home Missions of the Presbyterian Church in the USA, 1904), 29.

51. Methodist Episcopal Church, (Southern) California, 1881, 39–40.

52. Alice Hyson, "A Visit to One of Our Mission Schools," *Home Mission
Monthly,* November 1893, 9.

53. For detailed descriptions of *Penitente* practices from this perspective,
see Alexander Darley, *The Passionists of the Southwest, or the Holy Brotherhood: A Revelation of the 'Penitentes'* (Pueblo, Colo.) reprinted in *The Penitentes of New Mexico,* compiled by Carlos Cortés (New York: Arno Press,
1893); and Charles B. Sumner, "The Penitentes in New Mexico," *The Home
Missionary* 58, no. 7 (1885): 246–48. For a more sympathetic description of
the Penitentes see Marta Weigle, *Brothers of Light, Brothers of Blood: The
Penitentes of the Southwest* (University of New Mexico Press, 1976).

54. Congregational Church, New Mexico and Arizona General Association, Minutes of the Association Session, 1886, 317–18.

55. Emily Harwood, "Field and Work of the New Mexico Spanish Methodist Episcopal Mission," reprinted from "Gospel in All Lands" (1901), in *Life of Mrs. Emily J. Harwood,* by Harriet Kellogg (Albuquerque: El Abogado Press, 1903), 340.

56. Homer S. Thrall, correspondence to D. C. Kelley, published in the Annual Report of the Board of Missions of the Methodist Episcopal Church, South, 1878, 107.

57. Rankin, *Texas in 1850,* 55.

58. *Home Mission Monthly,* November 1892, 13.

59. *Home Mission Monthly,* November 1892, 10.

60. Allison, "Letter from Miss Allison," 318.

61. Bowman, "The Bishop's Letter," 292.

62. Baptist General Convention, Blanco Baptist Association, 1880, 6.

63. Baptist General Convention, Blanco Baptist Association, 1894, 8.

64. E. Harwood, "Field and Work," 334, 341; Kellogg, *Life of Emily Harwood,* 55, 225.

65. George M. Darley, *Pioneering in the San Juan* (Chicago: Fleming H. Revell, 1899), 172.

66. Rankin, *Twenty Years Among the Mexicans,* 23.

67. Presbyterian Church, United States of America, Board of Home Missions, Annual Report to the General Assembly, 1879, 9–10.

68. Richard Storrs, *Discourse in Behalf of the American Home Missionary Society* (New York: American Home Missionary Society, 1855), 12.

69. Rankin, *Texas in 1850,* 4.

70. Henry M. Storrs, "The Work and Attitude of the American Home Missionary Society," *The Home Missionary* 56, no. 9 (1882): 245.

71. John Menaul, *New Mexico and Its Claims, Briefly Presented by the Commissioner from the Presbytery of Santa Fé to the General Assembly of 1881* (Laguna, N.Mex.: Laguna Mission Press, 1881), 5.

72. Sherman H. Doyle, *Presbyterian Home Missions An Account of the Home Missions of the Presbyterian Church in the USA* (New York: Presbyterian Board of Home Missions, 1905), vi.

73. E. Harwood, "Field and Work," 333, 334.

74. Walter S. Scott, "Popular Meeting for Home Missions," *Trans-Mississippi Presbyterian*, May 26, 1898, 8; and Scott, "Mexicans in Texas," 133.

75. T. Harwood, *History of New Mexico . . . Missions,* 1:19.

76. Matilda A. Allison, "Mission Work in New Mexico," *Home Mission Monthly,* September 1887, 250.

77. Hyson, "A Visit," 9.

78. Emily Harwood, "The Mexicans of our Country" (1899), in *Life of Mrs. Emily J. Harwood,* by Harriet Kellogg (Albuquerque: El Abogado Press, 1903), 349.

79. Joseph B. Clark, *Leavening the Nation: The Story of American Home Missions* (New York: Baker and Taylor, 1903), 247.

80. Craig, *Our Mexicans,* 28.

81. T. Harwood, *History of New Mexico . . . Missions,* 1:52.

82. Emily Harwood, quoted in Kellogg, *Life of Emily Harwood,* 278.

83. Baptist General Convention, Texas, 1895, 25–26.

84. H. Kendall and Cyrus Dickson, "Appeal to Christian Women," *Rocky Mountain Presbyterian* 11, no. 12 (December 1880): 188.

85. Menaul, *New Mexico and Its Claims,* 6–7.

86. Charles Pomeroy, "Home Missions, New Mexico," *Presbyterian Home Missions* 10, no. 7 (July 1881): 324.

87. Emily Harwood in Kellogg, *Life of Emily Harwood,* 283.

88. Congregational Church Conference of New Mexico and Arizona, 1886, 318.

89. For a discussion of how Presbyterians perceived their ministry among the "exceptional populations" of the Southwest, see Banker, *Presbyterian Missions.*

Chapter 4

1. Red, *A History of the Presbyterian Church in Texas,* 379–80.

2. Brackenridge and García-Treto, *Iglesia Presbiteriana,* 2–8.

3. Red, *A History of the Presbyterian Church in Texas,* 72–74.

4. For details of her work, see Melinda Rankin, *Texas in 1850* (Boston: Damrell and Moore); and *Twenty Years Among the Mexicans: A Narrative of Missionary Labor* (St. Louis: Christian Publishing Company, 1875).

5. Hamilton Garmany Horton, documents in file, Southwest Texas Conference, United Methodist Church Archives, San Antonio, n.d., 1–2.

6. Methodist Episcopal Church, South, 1859, 171–72.

7. Ferenc Morton Szasz, *The Protestant Clergy in the Great Plains and Mountain West, 1865–1915* (Albuquerque: University of New Mexico Press, 1988), 134–35.

8. Lewis A. Meyers, *A History of New Mexico Baptists* (n.c.: The Baptist Convention of New Mexico, 1965), 48. Most of these people are later mentioned in MEC reports.

9. Ernest S. Stapleton, "The History of Baptist Missions in New Mexico 1849–1866" (master's thesis, University of New Mexico, 1954), 120–21.

10. Stapleton, "History of Baptist Missions in New Mexico," 30.

11. Meyers claims that Gonzales was baptized by immersion (*History of New Mexico Baptists,* 45–46).

12. Letter to American Baptist Home Mission Society, March 28, 1851, quoted in Stapleton, "History of Baptist Missions in New Mexico," 64.

13. T. Harwood, *History of New Mexico . . . Missions,* 1:48. Harwood states that many of those early converts maintained Baptist leanings, even though they joined the Methodists (1:202–4).

14. Thomas Harwood, "Connecting Links of History of the New Mexico Mission of the Methodist Episcopal Church," in Minutes of the 8th Session of the New Mexico Mission Conference of the Methodist Episcopal Church, 1883, 25.

15. T. Harwood, *History of New Mexico . . . Missions,* 1:44.

16. J. P. Durbin, "Report of the Missionary corresponding Secretary of New York [1855]," in *History of New Mexico Spanish and English Missions of the Methodist Episcopal Church from 1850–1910,* by Thomas Harwood (Albuquerque: El Abogado Press,1908), 1:34.

17. See Paul Horgan, *Lamy of Santa Fe: His Life and Times* (New York: Ferrar, Straus and Giroux, 1975).

18. Dalas D. Lore, correspondence to Corresponding Secretary, November 26, 1855, in T. Harwood, *History of New Mexico . . . Missions,* 1:37, 39.

19. T. Harwood, *History of New Mexico . . . Missions,* 1:49.

20. Ibid., 1:46–47.

21. Lela Weatherby, "A Study of the Early Years of the Presbyterian Work with the Spanish Speaking People of New Mexico and Colorado and its Development from 1850–1920" (master's thesis, Presbyterian College of Christian Education, Chicago, 1942), 20.

22. Leonard Pitt, *The Decline of the Californios: A Social History of the Spanish-Speaking Californians, 1846–1890* (Berkeley: University of California Press, 1970), 223. No other reference to this group or its impact has been found.

23. T. Harwood, *History of New Mexico . . . Missions,* 1:23.

CHAPTER 5

1. Hamilton Garmany Horton, documents in file, Southwest Texas Conference, United Methodist Church Archives, San Antonio, n.d., 5; Alfredo Náñez, *Historia de la Conferencia Río Grande de la Iglesia Metodista Unida* (Dallas: Bridwell Library, Southern Methodist University, 1981), 50.

2. Pablo García Verduzco, *Bosquejo Histórico del Metodismo Mexicano* (Nashville: Cokesbury Press, 1933), 17.

3. Methodist Episcopal Church, South, West Texas, 1883.

4. The churches were located in Bandera, Brakettville, Corpus Christi, Del Río, El Paso, Fort Davis, Graystown, Laredo, Lodi, Medina, Pecos, Río Grande City, Roma, San Antonio, and San Diego.

5. Methodist Episcopal Church, South, West Texas, 1877, 59.

6. *Texas Christian Advocate,* November 14, 1885, 4.

7. Ibid.

8. Alfredo Náñez, "Methodism Among the Spanish-Speaking People in Texas and New Mexico," in *One in the Lord: A History of Ethnic Minorities in the South Central Jurisdiction; The United Methodist Church,* by Walter Vernon, Alfredo Náñez, and John Graham (Oklahoma City: Commission on Archives and History, South Central Jurisdiction, The United Methodist Church, 1977), 62–63; Náñez, "English-Speaking and Spanish-Speaking Methodism—One" (paper presented to the Special San Antonio Area convocation on Missional Priorities, Travis Park United Methodist Church, San Antonio, October 5, 1978), 1.

9. One Spanish-speaking church was also begun in Phoenix, Arizona, by the Northwest Mexican Conference in 1892.

10. Home Mission Report, Presbyterian Church, United States, 1874, 18.

11. Brownsville was never included in any Texas statistical reports, and West Texas Presbytery minutes never mention the work there.

12. Spelled "Botelló," according to Brackenridge and García-Treto, *Iglesia Presbiteriana.*

13. Presbyterian Church, United States, Synod of Texas, 1894, 11.

14. Pratt is probably most well known for his translation of the Bible into the modern Spanish of his day. His *Versión Moderna* was used well into the twentieth century in parts of Latin America.

15. Brackenridge and García-Treto, *Iglesia Presbiteriana,* 25–27.

16. See Juan Martínez, "Origins and Development of Protestantism among Latinos in the Southwestern United States, 1836–1900" (Ph.D. diss., School of World Mission, Fuller Theological Seminary, 1996), Appendix 1, Statistical Table #4.

17. Scott, "Mexicans in Texas," 134–35.

18. Ibid., 134.

19. Ibid.

20. Ibid., 135.

21. Ibid., 137. The Latino Presbyterian congregations would continue to be financially dependent well into the twentieth century.

22. Baptist General Convention, Austin Baptist Association, quoted in Miller, "Texas Mexican Baptist History," 1.

23. Baptist General Convention, Blanco Baptist Convention, 1879, 2.

24. Baptist General Convention, Blanco Baptist Convention, 1880, 6.

25. Baptist General Convention, Blanco Baptist Convention, 1881, 7.

26. Baptist General Convention, Blanco Baptist Convention, 1882.

27. Baptist General Convention, Blanco Baptist Convention, 1884, 6.

28. It is not clear what these "former deeds of treachery" might be, though it could be a reference to the common, though false, understanding among many people in the United States that Mexico began the Mexican American War.

29. Baptist General Convention, Blanco Baptist Convention, 1885, 5.

30. See report of the Baptist General Convention, Texas, 1883. The first "Mexican" Baptist Church in Texas was started by a missionary from the Baptist work in Mexico.

31. Joshua Grijalva, *A History of Mexican Baptists in Texas, 1881–1981* (Dallas: Office of Language Missions, Baptist General Convention of Texas and Mexican Baptist Convention of Texas, 1982), 11–12. The Baptist historian B. F. Fuller states that the congregation in Laredo was organized in 1887 (*History of Texas Baptists* [Louisville, Ky.: Baptist Book Concern, 1900], 295). No statistical reports were never recorded for such a church in Baptist General Convention records, and minutes of the Blanco Baptist Association (which included the Laredo area) never mentioned it. There is no other record of a Mexican Baptist Church in Laredo until the turn of the century.

32. Baptist General Convention, San Antonio Baptist Association, 1888.

33. Methodist Episcopal Church, South, 1887, 80. Records of the Baptist General Convention (1888, 8) and the Baptist historian Fuller both state that Treviño was a Presbyterian (*History of Texas Baptists,* 295).

34. Powell met Treviño in Mexico while the latter was a MECS minister. Treviño asked for immersion baptism and joined the San Antonio church. This was the basis for Powell's recommendation, which was accepted by the State Board Baptist General Convention, Blanco Baptist Convention, 1888, 8.

35. Baptist General Convention, San Antonio Baptist Association, 1890.

36. Baptist General Convention, Texas, 1890, 19–20.

37. Baptist General Convention, Texas, 1891, 14.

38. Ibid.

39. Ibid.

40. Baptist General Convention, San Antonio Baptist Association, 1891, 34–35.

41. Fuller, *History of Texas Baptists,* 296; Miller, "Texas Mexican Baptist History," 8; Grijalva, *History of Mexican Baptists,* 18. MEC records describe a slightly different situation. Marchand was ordained by the MEC in 1886 (T. Harwood, *History of New Mexico . . . Missions,* 2:66). He pastored the El Paso MEC congregation in 1887, but was not its pastor when he decided to join the Baptists. MEC records do not record a significant membership loss in El Paso for the period in question.

42. Fuller, *History of Texas Baptists,* 296.

43. Baptist General Convention, San Antonio Baptist Association, 1892, 19.

44. Baptist General Convention, Texas, 1892, 12.

45. See Grijalva, *History of Mexican Baptists.*

46. Baptist General Convention, Texas, 1893, 11–12.

47. Ibid.

48. Ibid., 85.

49. Baptist General Convention, San Antonio Baptist Association, 1893, 21.

50. Fuller, *History of Texas Baptists,* 296.

51. Baptist General Convention, Texas, 1894, 24, 25, 11, and 1894 Statistical Table.

52. Baptist General Convention, Texas, 1895: Rio Grande Association, 10; quotation, 28.

53. See Miller, "Texas Mexican Baptist History," 8, 12, though he does not state when the El Paso church fell apart.

54. Fuller, *History of Texas Baptists,* 296; see list in Martínez, "Origins and Development," Appendix A, Statistical Table #5.

55. Miller, "Texas Mexican Baptist History," 10.

56. Ibid., 6.

57. See Martínez, "Origins and Development," Appendix A, Statistical Table #6.

58. Ibid.

59. *Survey of Service Organizations Represented in International Convention of Disciples of Christ* (St. Louis: Christian Board of Publications, 1928), 121–22.

60. The Latino Presbyterian Church in Brownsville was not a part of the West Texas Presbytery.

Chapter 6

1. Correspondence from Henry Kendall to Sheldon Jackson, July 18, 1870, quoted in Mark Banker, "Missionary to His Own People: José Ynés Perea and Hispanic Presbyterianism in New Mexico," unpublished manuscript; José Ynés Perea file (Albuquerque: Menaul Historical Library of the Southwest, n.d.), endnote 6.

2. Craig, *Our Mexicans,* 63.

3. See Weigle, *Brothers of Lights,* for an excellent introduction to the Penitentes. Alberto López Pulido looks at their development to the present in *The Sacred World of the Penitentes* (Smithsonian Institution Press, 2000).

4. *Neomejicano* Presbyterians, including several of Romero's direct descendants, claim that Romero was Martínez' illegitimate son (see R. Douglas Brackenridge and Francisco O. García-Treto, *Iglesia Presbiteriana: A History of Presbyterians and Mexican Americans in the Southwest* (San Antonio: Trinity University Press, 1974], 45; and Anonymous, "Padre Martínez—Forerunner of Taos Presbyterianism," *Menaul Historical Review* 9, no. 1 [1982]: 3). Accord-

ing to the Presbyterians, the fact that Romero joined them strengthened their efforts among the *Penitentes*. Ray John de Aragón strongly denies that Martínez had illegitimate children ("Padre Antonio José Martínez: The Man and the Myth," in *Padre Martínez: New Perspectives from Taos*, ed. E. A. Mares, 125–51 [Taos: Millicent Rogers Museum, 1988]). Walker (*Protestantism in the Sangre de Cristos*, p. 95) refers to Romero as one of Martínez's followers. Yohn (*A Contest of Faiths*, p. 71) calls Romero a relative of Padre Martínez.

5. Presbyterian Church, United States of America, Board of Home Missions, 1879, 11–12.

6. Quoted in Weatherby, "Early Years of the Presbyterian Work," 31. See Presbyterian Church, United States of America, Board of Home Missions, 1879, 9–10.

7. Matilda Allison, "Letter from Miss Allison," 318.

8. Craig, *Our Mexicans*, 69. For a complete list of Protestant schools established during the nineteenth century in the Southwest, see Appendix C in Juan Martínez, "Origins and Development of Protestantism among Latinos in the Southwestern United States, 1836–1900" (Ph.D. diss., School of World Mission, Fuller Theological Seminary, 1996).

9. According to Thomas Harwood, a Methodist missionary, one of the Presbyterian missionaries once told him that "we are waiting to see how your ordained men come out before we ordain many of ours" (*History of New Mexico . . . Missions*, 2:93).

10. James Gilchrist was also important to the work in New Mexico because he began the publication of the Presbyterian Spanish-language paper, *El Anciano*, which later became *La Aurora*.

11. Weatherby, "Early Years of the Presbyterian Work," 40.

12. More will be said about this institution in the section on Colorado.

13. Weatherby, "Early Years of the Presbyterian Work," 28.

14. For a complete listing of pastoral assignments, see Appendices B and D in Martínez, "Origins and Development."

15. See Statistical Table in Appendix.

16. For exact details see Statistical Table #1 in Martínez, "Origins and Development."

17. T. Harwood, *History of New Mexico . . . Missions*, 204.

18. Ibid., 1:48.

19. Most of this section is drawn from Thomas Harwood's memoirs, and other writings, though there are also some quotations from Emily Harwood's biography.

20. T. Harwood, *History of New Mexico . . . Missions*, 1:242.

21. Ibid. 1:19–20; Emily Harwood, "Field and Work of the New Mexico Spanish Methodist Episcopal Mission," reprinted from "Gospel in All Lands" (1901), in Kellogg, *Life of Mrs. Emily J. Harwood*, by Harriet Kellogg, 339.

22. T. Harwood, *History of New Mexico . . . Missions*, 1:213, 253.

23. Ibid., 1:178.

24. Ibid., 1:225.

25. Ibid., 206.

26. Emily Harwood, "The Mexicans of Our Country," reprinted from *New York Christian Advocate* (1901), in Kellogg, *Life of Mrs. Emily J. Harwood*, 346.

27. T. Harwood, *History of New Mexico . . . Missions*, 1:215, 251.

28. Kellogg, *Life of Mrs. Emily J. Harwood*, 134–35.

29. T. Harwood, *History of New Mexico . . . Missions*, 1:211.

30. Ibid., 215.

31. Ibid., 177–78.

32. T. Harwood, *History of New Mexico . . . Missions*, 1:19.

33. Ibid., 89. Harwood spends several pages of his memoirs describing this event.

34. Ibid., 205.

35. Kellogg, *Life of Emily Harwood*, 102.

36. T. Harwood, *History of New Mexico . . . Missions*, 1:76–77.

37. Ibid., 180.

38. T. Harwood, *History of New Mexico . . . Missions*, 1:187, 208.

39. For example, T. Harwood, *History of New Mexico . . . Missions*, 1:343–45.

40. See, for example, T. Harwood, *History of New Mexico . . . Missions*, 1:148, 180–81, 187; 2:198–99.

41. See, for example, T. Harwood, *History of New Mexico . . . Missions*, 1:362; 2:202–3.

42. Ibid., 1:170.

43. Thomas Harwood, "Connecting Links of History of the New Mexico Mission of the Methodist Episcopal Church," in Minutes of the 8th Session of the New Mexico Mission Conference of the Methodist Episcopal Church, 1883, 27.

44. T. Harwood, *History of New Mexico . . . Missions*, 1:52–53.

45. Ibid., 1:201–2.

46. Ibid., 1:199.

47. Ibid., 1:181–82.

48. T. Harwood, "Connecting Links," 28.

49. T. Harwood, *History of New Mexico . . . Missions*, 1:171–72.

50. Ibid., 1:209.

51. Ibid., 1:211.

52. Ibid.

53. Methodist Episcopal Church, New Mexico Mission Conference, 1883, 8.

54. T. Harwood, *History of New Mexico . . . Missions,* 1:246.

55. Methodist Episcopal Church, New Mexico Mission Conference, 1883, 22.

56. Ibid., 2:171–72, 327.

57. Ibid., 2: 359–60.

58. Ibid., 2: 43, 44. An interesting, though failed, ministry effort was the forming of a Methodist colony. *Neomejicano* Protestants often felt isolated and even persecuted at the hands of the Catholic majority. In 1888 a group of families, under the leadership of Rev. Lechoneus Frampton, formed a colony and church somewhere near Wagon Mound (exact location unknown; it does not appear on census maps of the period). The community, known as Framptonville, broke up by the beginning of the twentieth century and this type of effort was never repeated (Ibid., 2:88).

59. Ibid., 1:357.

60. E. Harwood, "Field and Work," 341.

61. T. Harwood, *History of New Mexico . . . Missions,* 1:175–76, 364–65; 2:91–93. The data used for these comparisons was never specified. In the 1888 report Harwood stated the basis of his comparison: "Counting the cost of Mission funds from 1872 to 1888, less the value of church property acquired during this time, also less the benevolent collections returned to their respective boards, the ratios stand as follows per cost of each member and probationer. The New Mexico Spanish one. The New Mexico English, *three;* Mexico, six; South America, six and a half" (I:365). Walker analyzes official MEC records and finds that Harwood's report does not stand up to careful scrutiny. According to Walker it cost Methodists "about three and one-half times as much for a Hispanic member as for an English member and five times as much for a Hispanic Church" (*Protestantism in the Sangre de Cristos,* p. 64).

62. Thomas Bowman, "The Bishop's Letter," Peralta, N.M., District Conference, June 20, 1877, in *History of New Mexico Spanish and English Missions of the Methodist Episcopal Church from 1850–1910,* by Thomas Harwood (Albuquerque: El Abogado Press, 1908), 294.

63. Ibid., 292. Missionaries often repeated statements such as this one quoted by Thomas Harwood in their correspondence with mission agencies and publications in the East.

64. T. Harwood, *History of New Mexico . . . Missions,* 1:210.

65. E. Harwood, "Field and Work," 333.

66. E. Harwood, "Mexicans of Our Country [1899]," 350.

67. E. Harwood, "Field and Work," 333–34.

68. T. Harwood, *History of New Mexico . . . Missions,* 1:229–30.

69. Ibid., 1:176.

70. Ibid., 1:161.

71. E. Harwood, "Mexicans of Our Country [1899]," 349.

72. E. Harwood, "Mexicans of Our Country [1901]," 342.

73. T. Harwood, *History of New Mexico . . . Missions,* 2:75.

74. E. Harwood, "Mexicans of Our Country [1899]," 348.

75. Kellogg, *Life of Emily Harwood,* 55.

76. T. Harwood, *History of New Mexico . . . Missions,* 2:90.

77. Ibid., 2:10–11.

78. J. M. Ashley, "Progress in New Mexico," *The Home Missionary* 54, no. 11 (March 1882): 309.

79. J. M. Ashley, "The Work in New Mexico and Arizona," *The Home Missionary* 55, no. 5 (February 1883): 205–6, 208.

80. Congregational Church, New Mexico, 1884.

81. J. M. Ashley, "A New-Mexican Trip," *The Home Missionary* 56, no. 10 (February 1884): 396.

82. Charles B. Sumner, "New Mexico and Arizona," *The Home Missionary* 58, no. 3 (1885): 111; and "The Penitentes in New Mexico," *The Home Missionary* 58, no. 7 (1885): 246.

83. Congregational Church, New Mexico, 1888.

84. Congregational Church, New Mexico, 1890.

85. E. Lyman Hood, "New Mexico and Arizona," *The Home Missionary* 64, no. 3 (July 1891): 138–39.

86. See "The Hidden Idol," *The Home Missionary* 61, no. 4 (August 1888): 193.

87. *The Home Missionary,* Baptist General Convention, Texas, 1891, 139.

88. Congregational Church, New Mexico, 1886, 318.

89. *The Home Missionary* 59, no. 7 (November 1886): 280.

90. *The Home Missionary* 61, no. 4 (August 1888): 193.

91. Horacio Ladd, "University of New Mexico, Santa Fé, N.M." December 20, 1881, document in the Horacio Oliver Ladd File, University Library, University of New Mexico, Albuquerque.

92. Ibid.

93. Five in 1885, six in 1890, and eight in 1900; Walker, *Protestantism in the Sangre de Cristos,* pp. 66, 67, 79.

94. Ashley, "Progress in New Mexico"; Ezequiel Chávez, "Quarterly Report to Joseph B. Clark, Secretary of the AHMS, April 30, 1893" (American Home Missionary Society Records, New Mexico File, Amistad Research Center, New Orleans, Louisiana).

95. See Statistical Table in the Appendix. For the sake of comparison with other denominations the following numbers are used: 1891: 11; 1892: 15; 1893: 19; 1894: 23; 1895: 27; 1896: 31; 1897: 35; 1898: 38; 1899: 42; 1900: 45; though only the first number is based on a statistical report. Some growth

is assumed from a report by Chávez in 1893 in which he mentioned two people, and possibly two others, being received into the church ("Quarterly Report to Joseph B. Clark," 2–4).

96. Congregational Church, New Mexico, 1909.

97. Ibid.

98. T. Harwood, *History of New Mexico . . . Missions,* 1:202–4.

99. Andrew E. Murray, *The Skyline Synod: Presbyterianism in Colorado and Utah* (Denver: Golden Bell Press, 1971), 64.

100. Walker analyzes this issue in her chapter on "Americanization and Catholic Reaction" in *Protestantism in the Sangre de Cristos,* pp. 89–106.

101. Moore, "Life of Mrs. Emily Jane Harwood," i; see also T. Harwood, *History of New Mexico . . . Missions,* 1:242; and Sumner, "Penitentes in New Mexico," 246.

102. Ibid., 340.

103. More will be said about *neomejicano* Bibles in chapter eight.

104. See Walker, *Protestantism in the Sangre de Cristos,* for a description of this process.

CHAPTER 7

1. Darley played an important role in Presbyterian ministry among the Spanish speaking. He was a missionary assigned by the Pueblo (Colorado) Presbytery who took an interest in working among Latinos and began learning Spanish. In the early 1880s he published a small Spanish language paper, *El Anciano.* He fell out of favor with the Presbytery due to financial problems and tensions with presbytery and synod leaders. But he continued working among the Spanish-speaking and would later plant a church in Pueblo and publish another periodical, *La Hermandad.*

2. Weatherby, 51. This is why the Costilla, New Mexico, church was a part of the Pueblo Presbytery of the Colorado Synod; it had originally been organized in Colorado.

3. George M. Darley, *Pioneering in the San Juan* (Chicago: Fleming H. Revell, 1899), 173.

4. Weatherby, "Early Years of the Presbyterian Work," 50.

5. Norman J. Bender provides a useful analysis of the reasons for the college's failure in "A College Where One Ought to Be," *The Colorado Magazine* 49, no. 3 (1972): 196–218.

6. Andrew E. Murray, *The Skyline Synod: Presbyterianism in Colorado and Utah* (Denver: Golden Bell Press, 1971), 37.

7. See Statistical Table #8 in Martínez, "Origins and Development of Protestantism among Latinos."

8. Ibid., Statistical Tables #7 and #8.

9. See excursus on the Bible in *Neomejicano* Protestant Folklore in Chapter 8.

10. See Alexander Darley, *The Passionists of the Southwest, or the Holy Brotherhood: A Revelation of the 'Penitentes'* (Pueblo, Colo.) reprinted in *The Penitentes of New Mexico,* compiled by Carlos Cortés (New York: Arno Press, 1893).

11. See Statistical Table #9 in Martínez, "Origins and Development."

12. Craig, *Our Mexicans,* 67–68.

13. See Statistical Table #10 in Martínez, "Origins and Development."

14. C. V. Anthony, *Fifty Years of Methodism: A History of the Methodist Episcopal Church Within the Bounds of the California Annual Conference from 1847–1897* (San Francisco: Methodist Book Concern, 1901).

15. Ibid., 14.

16. Methodist Episcopal Church, Northern California Conference, 1879, 22.

17. Methodist Episcopal Church, (Southern) California Conference, 1880, 17–18.

18. Methodist Episcopal Church, (Southern) California Conference, 1881, 33.

19. Ibid., 39–40.

20. Ibid., 50.

21. Methodist Episcopal Church, (Southern) California Conference, 1882, 22.

22. Ibid., 23. The national statistical report only lists a membership total of 37 for Los Angeles.

23. Ibid., 24–25. The report does not explain what a "band" is. It only contrasts this with the MEC goal of getting Latinos to be a part of a MEC church.

24. Methodist Episcopal Church, (Southern) California Conference, 1883, 31.

25. Methodist Episcopal Church, (Southern) California Conference, 1889, 58.

26. Eduard Arther Wicher, *The Presbyterian Church in California, 1849–1927* (New York: Frederick H. Hitchcock, The Grafton Press, 1927), 305. Wicher mentions a reference to the organization of a Spanish church in San Francisco in 1883, but states that "it disappeared almost immediately from the roll of the presbytery" (306).

27. Presbyterian Church, United States of America, General Assembly, 1883, 1041.

28. Wicher, *Presbyterian Church in California,* 306–7.

29. See Statistical Tables #12 and #13 in Martínez, "Origins and Development."

30. Women's Home Missionary Society, Presbyterian Church, USA, California, 1894, 6.

31. See Statistical Table #12 in Martínez, "Origins and Development."

32. Clarence Lokey, "In the Great Southwest Texas, New Mexico, Arizona and California," in *Spanish Doorways: American Methodists and the Evangelical Mission Among Spanish-Speaking Neighbors* (New York: World Outlook Press, 1964), 80–81.

33. Leonard Pitt, *The Decline of the Californios: A Social History of the Spanish-Speaking Calfiornians, 1846–1890* (Berkeley: University of California Press, 1966), 43.

Chapter 8

1. Emily Harwood, "Field and Work," 335.

2. Ibid., 340.

3. Mark Banker, "Missionary to His Own People: José Ynés Perea and Hispanic Presbyterianism in New Mexico," unpublished manuscript, José Ynés Perea file (Albuquerque: Menaul Historical Library of the Southwest, n.d.), 20.

4. Reynaldo Avila, *La Verdad y el Error,* published tract (Victoria, Tex.: The Texas Guide, 1904); James S. Maverick, *José Policarpo Rodríguez: His Life in His Own Words* (Nashville: Publishing House of the Methodist Episcopal Church, n.d.), 104–9.

5. Pablo García Verduzco, *Bosquejo Histórico del Metodismo Mexicano* (Nashville: Cokesbury Press 1933), 17.

6. Maverick, *José Policarpo Rodríguez,* 94–97; José Ynés Perea, correspondence to Norman Skinner, January 19, 1897, Pajarito, N.M., José Ynés Perea File, Menaul Historical Library of the Southwest, Albuquerque; Edith Agnew, *Hand on My Shoulder* (New York: Board of National Missions, The United Presbyterian Church in the USA, 1953), 52.

7. Weatherby, "Early Years of the Presbyterian Work," 28.

8. Thomas Bowman, "The Bishop's Letter," Peralta, N.M., District Conference, June 20, 1877, in T. Harwood, *History of New Mexico . . . Missions,* 1:292.

9. Walker, *Protestantism in the Sangre de Cristos,* 115.

10. Harwood, "Field and Work," 341.

11. Ibid.; Kellogg, *Life of Emily Harwood,* 304.

12. Thomas Harwood, *History of the New Mexico . . . Missions,* 51.

13. Kellogg, *Life of Emily Harwood,* 278.

14. Alfredo Mirandé, *The Chicano Experience: An Alternative Perspective* (South Bend, Ind.: University of Notre Dame Press, 1985), 17–47.

15. Kellogg, *Life of Emily Harwood,* 303.

16. See Randi Walker, *Protestantism in the Sangre de Cristos,* for a description of this process of decline.

17. Weatherby, "Early Years of the Presbyterian Work," 33.

18. Eduard Arther Wicher, *The Presbyterian Church in California,* 307–8; Weatherby, "Early Years of the Presbyterian Work," 40.

19. Wicher, *Presbyterian Church in California,* 306).

20. Weatherby, "Early Years of the Presbyterian Work," 48–49.

21. T. Harwood, *History of New Mexico . . . Missions,* 1:148; Weatherby, "Early Years of the Presbyterian Work," 53.

22. See Banker, "Missionary to His Own People."

23. T. Harwood, *History of New Mexico . . . Missions,* 1:202–3, 343–44.

24. Ibid., 2:292–95.

25. Joshua Grijalva, *A History of Mexican Baptists in Texas,* 15.

26. The material in this section formed the basis for a published article: "The Bible in Novomejicano Protestant Folklore," *Apuntes* 17, no. 1 (Spring 1997).

27. Ferenc Morton Szasz, *The Protestant Clergy,* 142.

28. Edith Agnew, "A Treasured Bible," *El Farolero* 5, no. 4 (1972): 1.

29. "The History of a Bible," *The Home Missionary* 60, no. 8 (December 1887): 330–31.

30. Francis M. Gilchrist, "Our Work for Spanish-Speaking People," *The Church at Home and Abroad,* February 1897, 122. According to Gilchrist, this Bible was published in 1828 (ibid.).

31. Julia Jaramillo Romack, "Story of the Gomez Bible," *The Menaul Historical Review* 6, no. 2 (1979): 5.

32. Brackenridge and García-Treto, *Iglesia Presbiteriana,* 34–35.

33. This Bible would later be donated by the family to the Menaul Historical Library; Agnew, "A Treasured Bible," 1.

34. Dora Ortiz Vásquez, "Story of the Ocaté Bible," in *Sowers Went Forth,* by Ruth Barber and Edith Agnew (Albuquerque: Menaul Historical Library of the Southwest, 1981), 26.

35. Thomas Harwood, "Connecting Links of History of the New Mexico Mission of the Methodist Episcopal Church," in Minutes of the 8th Session of the New Mexico Mission Conference of the Methodist Episcopal Church, 1883, 26.

36. Gilchrist, "Our Work for Spanish-Speaking People," 122.

37. The numbers used are based on the Statistical Table in the Appendix and refer to the adult members reported by the Latino congregations. These numbers do not include children or "sympathizers" (people who attended Protestant churches but had not made a commitment to become members). Adult members needed to publicly confess their Protestant faith, make a com-

mitment to the local congregation, and in the case of Baptists and Disciples, accept immersion baptism.

38. The summary in this paragraph and the next is based on data available in the statistical tables in Juan Martínez, "Origins and Development of Protestantism among Latinos in the Southwestern United States, 1836–1900" (Ph.D. diss., School of World Mission, Fuller Theological Seminary, 1996). Membership totals for 1870–1900 are reported in the statistical table in the Appendix.

39. For a complete list of the congregations see the statistical tables in Martínez, "Origins and Development."

CONCLUSION

1. Luis D. León, *La Llorona's Children: Religion, Life and Death in the U.S.-Mexican Borderlands* (Berkeley: University of California Press, 2004), 235.

2. Walker, *Protestantism in the Sangre de Cristos*, 109.

3. See, for example, Albert Camarillo, *Chicanos in a Changing Society: From Mexican Pueblos to American Barrios in Santa Barbara and Southern California, 1848–1930* (Cambridge: Harvard University Press, 1979); Arnoldo de León and Kenneth L. Stewart, *Tejanos and the Numbers Game: A Socio-Historical Interpretation from the Federal Censuses, 1850–1900* (Albuquerque: University of New Mexico Press, 1982); David Montejano, *Anglos and Mexicans in the Making of Texas, 1836–1986* (Austin: University of Texas Press, 1987); and Thomas E. Sheridan, *Los Tucsonenses: The Mexican Community in Tucson, 1854–1941* (Tucson: University of Arizona Press, 1986).

Bibliography

Denominational Records

Baptist Association, Worchester, New York. Minutes of the 16th Anniversary, 1846.

Baptist General Convention, Blanco (Texas) Association. Minutes of the Annual Sessions, 1880–1901.

Baptist General Convention, San Antonio (Texas) Association. Minutes of the Annual Sessions, 1888–1901.

Baptist General Convention, Texas Association. Proceedings of the Annual Sessions, 1888–1895.

Congregational Ministries and Church in Vermont. Extracts from the Minutes of the General Convention Session, 1847.

Congregational Church, First Church of Albuquerque, New Mexico. Membership Manual, 1892.

Congregational Church, New Mexico and Arizona General Association. Minutes of the Association Sessions, 1884–1909.

Methodist Episcopal Church, Minutes of the Annual Conference, 1870–1900.

Methodist Episcopal Church (Southern) California Conference. Minutes of the Annual Conference, 1880–1895.

Methodist Episcopal Church, New Mexico Mission Conference. Minutes of the Annual Conference, 1883, 1884.

Methodist Episcopal Church, Northern California Conference. Minutes of the Annual Conference, 1880.

Methodist Episcopal Church, South, Minutes of the Annual Conference, 1851, 1870–1900.

Methodist Episcopal Church, South, Rio Grande Mission Conference. Minutes of the Annual Conference, 1859–1863.

Methodist Episcopal Church, South, Rio Grande Conference. Minutes of the Annual Conference, 1864–1866.

Methodist Episcopal Church, South, West Texas Conference. Minutes of the Annual Conference, 1866–1985.

Presbyterian Church, United States. Minutes of the General Assembly, 1874, 1888–1900.

Presbyterian Church, United States, Presbytery of Western Texas. Excerpts of the Minutes of the Presbytery, 1884–1887.

Presbyterian Church, United States, Synod of Texas. Minutes of the Annual Session, 1894.

Presbyterian Church, United States of America. Minutes of the General Assembly, 1846, 1870–1900.

Presbyterian Church, United States of America. Board of Home Missions. Annual Reports to the General Assembly 1877, 1879.

Presbyterian Church, United States of America, Presbytery of Santa Fe. Minutes of the Presbytery, 1875–1895.

Presbyterian Church, United States of America, Synod of California. Woman's Synodical Society of Home Missions, 1894, 1900.

Presbyterian Church, United States of America, Synod of New Mexico, 1891.

Protestant Episcopal Church in the United States of America, Maryland. Journal of the 59th Annual Convention, 1847.

Periodicals

El Abogado Cristiano Neo-Mexicano

El Anciano

La Aurora

The Baptist Missionary Magazine

Christian Register

The Field Is the World

La Hermandad

Home Mission Monthly

The Home Missionary

Massachusetts Quarterly Review

Methodist Almanac

El Metodista

Metodista Neo-Mexicano

El Obrero Cristiano

Presbyterian Home Missions

Revista Evangélica

Rocky Mountain Presbyterian

Southern Presbyterian Review

Texas Christian Advocate

The Texas Methodist Historical Quarterly

Trans-Mississippi Presbyterian

United States Magazine and Democratic Review

Contemporary Sources

American Home Missionary Society. Reports presented by the Executive Committee, 1846, 1847.

———. "Present Relative Position." Report printed with "Home Missions," a Sermon in behalf of the American Home Missionary Society, p. 48. New York: American Home Missionary Society, 1849.

Anthony, C. V. *Fifty Years of Methodism: A History of the Methodist Episcopal Church Within the Bounds of the California Annual Conference from 1847–1897.* San Francisco: Methodist Book Concern, 1901.

Armendáriz, Trinidad. Letters to Alexander Sutherland. January 28 and February 12, 1878. Published in the Annual Report of the Board of Home Missions of the Methodist Episcopal Church, South, pp. 113–15. Nashville: Southern Methodist Publishing House, 1878.

Avila, Reynaldo. *La Verdad y el Error.* Published tract. Victoria, Tex.: The Texas Guide, 1904. Walter Scott File, Stitt Library, Austin Presbyterian Seminary, Austin, Texas.

Barnes, Albert. "Home Missions." A Sermon in behalf of the American Home Missionary Society. New York: William Osborn, for the American Home Missionary Society, 1849.

Bowman, Thomas. "The Bishop's Letter." Peralta, N.M. District Conference, June 20, 1877. In *History of New Mexico Spanish and English Missions of the Methodist Episcopal Church from 1850–1910,* by Thomas Harwood, pp. 291–96. Albuquerque: El Abogado Press, 1908.

Calhoun, John C. "The Government of a White Race." In *The Congressional Globe,* 30th Congress, First Session, pp. 98–99. Reprinted in *Foreigners in their Native Land: Historical Roots of the Mexican Americans,* ed. David J. Weber, pp. 135–37. Albuquerque: University of New Mexico Press, 1848.

Chávez, Ezequiel. "Quarterly Report to Joseph B. Clark, Secretary of the A. H. M. S., April 30, 1893." American Home Missionary Society Records, New Mexico File, Amistad Research Center, New Orleans, Louisiana.

Clark, Joseph B. *Leavening the Nation: The Story of American Home Missions.* New York: The Baker & Taylor Company, 1903.

Craig, Robert M. *Our Mexicans.* New York: The Board of Home Missions of the Presbyterian Church in the USA, 1904.

Darley, Alexander. *The Passionists of the Southwest, or The Holy Brotherhood: A Revelation of the 'Penitentes'.* Pueblo, Colorado. Reprinted in *The Penitentes of New Mexico.* Compiled by Carlos Cortés. New York: Arno Press, 1893.

Darley, George M. *Pioneering in the San Juan.* Chicago: Fleming H. Revell Company, 1899.

Davis, W. W. H. *El Gringo, or New Mexico and Her People.* 1857. Reprinted, Santa Fe: Rydal Press, 1938.

Doyle, Sherman H. *Presbyterian Home Missions: An Account of the Home Missions of the Presbyterian Church in the U.S.A.* New York: Presbyterian Board of Home Missions, 1905.

Durbin, J. P. Report of the Missionary Corresponding Secretary of New York, 1855. In *History of New Mexico Spanish and English Missions of the Methodist Episcopal Church from 1850–1910,* by Thomas Harwood, p. 34. Albuquerque: El Abogado Press, 1908.

Forrester, H. Report from New Mexico and Arizona to the Domestic Committee of the Board of Missions of the Protestant Episcopal Church in the United States of America, 1877.

Fuller, B. F. *History of Texas Baptists.* Louisville, Ky.: Baptist Book Concern, 1900.

García, Benito. "Memoirs—Mrs. Ana María Rael García." In The Minutes of the 9th Session of the New Mexico Mission Conference of the Methodist Episcopal Church, 1884, p. 46. Las Vegas, N.M.: Daily Optic Print, 1884.

Gilchrist, Francis M. "Our Work for Spanish-Speaking People." *The Church at Home and Abroad,* February 1897, pp. 121–23. Reprinted by the Board of Education, Joseph James Gilchrist File. Menaul Historical Library of the Southwest. Albuquerque, N.M.

Goodykoontz, Colin Brummitt. *Home Missions on the American Frontier.* Caldwell, Idaho: The Caxton Printers, 1939.

Harris, Samuel. "The Mexican War." A Sermon delivered on the Annual Thanksgiving at Conway, Mass., November 26, 1846. Greenfield: Merriam and Mirick, Printers, 1847.

Hart, Burdett. "Better Things than War." A discourse delivered at the Congregational Church in Faith Haven on the Annual Thanksgiving of 1847. New Haven: Peck & Stafford, Printers, 1847.

Harwood, Emily. "Field and Work of the New Mexico Spanish Methodist Episcopal Mission." Reprinted from "Gospel in All Lands" (1901). In *Life of Mrs. Emily J. Harwood,* by Harriet Kellogg, pp. 330–43. Albuquerque: El Abogado Press, 1903.

———. "The Mexicans of Our Country [1899]." In *Life of Mrs. Emily J. Harwood,* by Harriet Kellogg, pp. 348–51. Albuquerque: El Abogado Press, 1903.

———. "The Mexicans of Our Country [1901]." Reprinted from *New York Christian Advocate.* In *Life of Mrs. Emily J. Harwood,* by Harriet Kellogg, pp. 344–46. Albuquerque: El Abogado Press, 1903.

Harwood, Thomas. "Connecting Links of History of the New Mexico Mission of the Methodist Episcopal Church." In the Minutes of the 8th Session of the New Mexico Mission Conference of the Methodist Episcopal Church, 1883. Las Vegas, N.M.: Daily Optic Print, 1883.

———. *History of the New Mexico Spanish and English Missions of the Methodist Episcopal Church from 1850–1910.* 2 vols. Albuquerque: El Abogado Press, 1908.

———. "Memoirs—Rev. Ambrozio C. Gonzales." In the Minutes of the 9th Session of the New Mexico Mission Conference of the Methodist Episcopal Church, 1884, pp. 36–39. Las Vegas, N.M.: Daily Optic Print, 1884.

———. "Memoirs—Rev. José Santos Telles." In the Minutes of the 9th Session of the New Mexico Mission Conference of the Methodist Episcopal Church, 1884, pp. 39–41. Las Vegas, N.M.: Daily Optic Print, 1884.

Hodge, Charles, "Narrative on the State of Religion." In the Minutes of the General Assembly of the Presbyterian Church in the United States of America, 1846, 220–30.

Horton, Hamilton Garmany. Documents File. n.d. Southwest Texas Conference, United Methodist Church Archives. San Antonio.

Jay, William. *A Review of the Causes and Consequences of the Mexican War.* Boston: Benjamin B. Mussey & Company, 1849.

Kellogg, Harriet. *Life of Mrs. Emily J. Harwood.* Albuquerque: El Abogado Press, 1903.

Ladd, Horacio. Extracts from his autobiography. n.d. Horacio Oliver Ladd File. University Library, University of New Mexico, Albuquerque.

————. "University of New Mexico, Santa Fé, N.M." December 20, 1881. Horacio Oliver Ladd File. University Library, University of New Mexico, Albuquerque.

Livermore, Abiel Abbot. *The War with Mexico Revisited.* Boston: The American Peace Society, 1850.

Lore, Dalas D. Correspondence to Corresponding Secretary of the Mission Society, November 26, 1855. In *History of New Mexico: Spanish and English Missions of the Methodist Episcopal Church from 1850–1910,* by Thomas Harwood, pp. 37–39. Albuquerque: El Abogado Press, 1908.

Mason, Erskine. "An Evangelical Ministry, the Security of a Nation." A Sermon preached on behalf of the American Home Missionary Society, January 8, 1848. New York: William Osborn, 1848.

Maverick, James S. *José Policarpo Rodríguez: His Life in His Own Words.* Nashville: Publishing House of the Methodist Episcopal Church, South, n.d. (probably published 1914).

Menaul, John. *New Mexico and Its Claims, Briefly Presented by the Commissioner from the Presbytery of Santa Fé to the General Assembly of 1881.* Laguna, N.M.: Laguna Mission Press, 1881.

————. "Report in the Minutes of the Annual Conference of the Synod of New Mexico." Presbyterian Church in the United States of America, 1891, p. 8.

Miter, John J. "Address of Rev. J. J. Miter, Milwaukee, Wisconsin." In The 20th Report of the American Home Missionary Society, pp. 115–20. New York: William Osborn, 1846.

Moore, David H. "To the Life of Mrs. Emily Jane Harwood." In *Life of Mrs. Emily J. Harwood,* by Harriet Kellogg, pp. i–ii. Albuquerque: El Abogado Press, 1903.

Paz, Gumercindo. "Letters to Alexander Sutherland, February 7, 16, and 22, 1878." In the Annual Report of the Board of Missions of the Methodist Episcopal Church, South, pp. 110–13. Nashville: Southern Methodist Publishing House, 1878.

Peabody, A. P. "Ringing Bells for Victories in War." *Christian Register* 26, no. 23 (1847): 89.

Perea, José Ynés. Correspondence to Susan Gates, August 8, 1878,

Las Vegas, N.M. José Ynés Perea File. Menaul Historical Library of the Southwest. Menaul School, Albuquerque.

———. Correspondence to Norman Skinner, January 19, 1897, Pajarito, N.M. José Ynés Perea File. Menaul Historical Library of the Southwest. Menaul School, Albuquerque.

Phillips, William W. An address, delivered at Peekskill, New York, October 21, 1846, before the Synod of New York by their appointment, and published at their request. Board of Foreign Missions of the Presbyterian Church, 1846.

Putnam, Dr., "Allegiance to Government." *Christian Register* 26, no. 19 (1847): 74.

Rankin, Melinda, *Texas in 1850.* Boston: Damrell and Moore., 1850.

———. *Twenty Years Among the Mexicans: A Narrative of Missionary Labor.* St. Louis: Christian Publishing Company, 1875.

Read, Hollis. *The Hand of God in History, or Divine Providence Historically Illustrated in the Extension and Establishment of Christianity.* Hartford: H. E. Robins and Company, 1858.

Red, William Stuart. *A History of the Presbyterian Church in Texas.* Austin: The Steck Company, 1936.

Rendón, Gabino. "Don Ynés Perea." *La Aurora* 11, no. 22 (1910): 2.

Roberts, James M. "Northern New Mexican." *Rocky Mountain Presbyterian* 11, no. 2 (1880): 24.

Rodríguez, A. J. "Bendito aquel que muera en el Señor." *El Anciano,* January 10, 1894, p. 1.

Sánchez, J. Pablo. Funeral Address for Emily J. Harwood. In *Life of Mrs. Emily J. Harwood,* by Harriet Kellogg, pp. xiii–xvi. Albuquerque: El Abogado Press, 1903.

Sánchez, Manuel D. J. "Dios os guarde hasta otra vez." *El Anciano,* January 10, 1894, p. 1.

Scott, Walter S. "The Mexicans in Texas." In *At Our Door: A Study of Home Missions with Special Reference to the South and West,* by Samuel L. Morris, pp. 130–38. New York: Fleming H. Revell Company, 1904.

Smyth, Thomas. "The Relations of Christianity to War, and The Portraiture of a Christian Soldier." A discourse delivered on the occasion of the First Commencement of the Citadel Academy. Charleston, S.C.: B. Jenkins, 1847.

Storrs, Richard S. *Discourse in Behalf of the American Home Missionary Society.* New York: American Home Missionary Society, 1855.

Strong, Josiah. *Our Country: Its Possible Future and Its Present Crisis.* New York: The Baker and Taylor Company, 1858.

Sutherland, Alexander H. Correspondence to D. C. Kelley, February, 5, 1878. Published in the Annual Report of the Board of Missions of the Methodist Episcopal Church, South, 1878, pp. 108–10.

Teats, Mary E. "Introductory Note by the National Evangelist of the Women's Christian Temperance Union." In *Life of Mrs. Emily J. Harwood,* by Harriet Kellogg, pp. ii–vii. Albuquerque: El Abogado Press, 1903.

Thayer, W. M. "The New Mexican." *The Home Missionary,* March 1890, 492.

Thomas, Thomas E. "Covenant Breaking, and Its Consequences, or The Present Posture of Our National Affairs, in Connection with the Mexican War." Two discourses preached in Hamilton, Ohio, July 4 and 11, 1847. Rossville: J. M. Christy, Printer, 1847.

Thompson, Charles L. *The Soul of America: The Contribution of Presbyterian Home Missions.* New York: Fleming H. Revell Company, 1919.

Thrall, Homer S. *A Brief History of Methodism in Texas.* Nashville: Publishing House of the M.E. Church, South, 1894.

———. Correspondence to D. C. Kelley. Published in the Annual Report of the Board of Missions of the Methodist Episcopal Church, South, 1878, pp. 106–8.

Tilden, William P. "War: A Sermon Suggested by the Death of Lieut. Edward Eastman." *Christian Register* 26, no. 4 (1847): 10.

Winton, George B. "Mexican Missions at Home." *The Texas Methodist Historical Quarterly* 2, no. 1 (July 1910): 85–87.

Secondary Sources

Agnew, Edith. *Hand on My Shoulder.* New York: Board of National Missions, The United Presbyterian Church in the U.S.A., 1953.

———. "A Treasured Bible." *El Farolero* 5, no. 4 (1972): 1.

Agnew, Edith, and Ruth. K. Barber. "The Unique Presbyterian School System of New Mexico." *Journal of Presbyterian History* 49, no. 3 (1971): 197–221.

Anonymous. "Padre Martínez—Forerunner of Taos Presbyterianism." *Menaul Historical Review* 9, no. 1 (1982): 3.

Aragón, Ray John de. "Padre Antonio José Martínez: The Man and the Myth." In *Padre Martínez: New Perspectives from Taos*, ed. E. A. Mares, pp. 125–51. Taos: Millicent Rogers Museum, 1988.

Atkins Grainger, Jane, ed. *El Centenario de la Palabra: El Rito Presbyterian Church, 1879–1979, Chacón, New Mexico*. Albuquerque: Menaul Historical Library of the Southwest, 1980.

Banker, Mark. "Missionary to His Own People: José Ynés Perea and Hispanic Presbyterianism in New Mexico." Unpublished manuscript. José Ynés Perea File. Albuquerque: Menaul Historical Library of the Southwest, n.d.

———. *Presbyterian Missions and Cultural Interaction in the Far Southwest, 1850–1950*. Urbana: University of Illinois Press, 1993.

Barton, Paul. "In Both Worlds: A History of Hispanic Protestantism in the United States Southwest (Texas, New Mexico)." Ph.D. diss., Southern Methodist University, 1999.

Bender, Norman J. "A College Where One Ought to Be." *The Colorado Magazine* 49, no. 3 (1972): 196–218.

Billington, Ray Allen. *The Protestant Crusade, 1800–1860: A Study of the Origins of American Nativism*. Chicago: Quadrangle Books, 1964.

Bodo, John R. *The Protestant Clergy and Public Issues, 1812–1848*. Princeton: Princeton University Press, 1954.

Brackenridge, Douglas R., and Francisco O. García-Treto. *Iglesia Presbiteriana: A History of Presbyterians and Mexican Americans in the Southwest*. San Antonio: Trinity University Press, 1974.

Camarillo, Albert. *Chicanos in a Changing Society: From Mexican Pueblos to American Barrios in Santa Barbara and Southern California, 1848–1930*. Cambridge: Harvard University Press, 1979.

Chávez, John. *The Lost Land: The Chicano Image of the Southwest*. Albuquerque: University of New Mexico Press, 1984.

Ellsworth, Clayton Sumner. "American Churches and the Mexican War." *American Historical Review* 45, no. 2 (1940): 301–26.

García, Mario T. "The Californios of San Diego and the Politics of Accommodation, 1846–1860." *Aztlán* 6, no. 1 (1975): 69–85.

Garza, Minerva. "Datos Históricos La Trinidad Iglesia Metodista Unida." Unpublished document, 1983.

García Verduzco, Pablo. *Bosquejo Histórico del Metodismo Mexicano*. Nashville: Cokesbury Press, 1933.

Grijalva, Joshua. *A History of Mexican Baptists in Texas, 1881–1981*.

Dallas: Office of Language Missions, Baptist General Convention of Texas and Mexican Baptist Convention of Texas, 1982.

Horgan, Paul. *Lamy of Santa Fe: His Life and Times.* New York: Ferrar, Straus & Giroux, 1975.

Jaramillo Romack, Julia. "Story of the Gomez Bible." *The Menaul Historical Review* 6, no. 2 (1979): 5.

León, Arnoldo de, and Kenneth L. Stewart. *Tejanos and the Numbers Game: A Socio-Historical Interpretation from the Federal Censuses, 1850–1900.* Albuquerque: University of New Mexico Press, 1989.

León, Luis D. *La Llorona's Children Religión, Life and Death in the U.S.-Mexican Borderlands.* Berkeley: University of California Press, 2004.

Lokey, Clarence. "In the Great Southwest Texas, New Mexico, Arizona, and California." In *Spanish Doorways: American Methodists and the Evangelical Mission among Spanish-Speaking Neighbors,* pp. 59–86. New York: World Outlook Press, 1964.

Martínez, Juan. "Origins and Development of Protestantism among Latinos in the Southwestern United States, 1836–1900." Ph.D. diss., School of World Mission, Fuller Theological Seminary, 1996.

Merk, Frederick. *Manifest Destiny and Mission in American History: A Reinterpretation.* New York: Vintage Books, 1966.

Meyers, Lewis A. *A History of New Mexico Baptists.* n.c.: The Baptist Convention of New Mexico, 1965.

Miller, William Bricen. "Texas Mexican Baptist History, or A History of Baptist Work among Mexicans in Texas." Ph.D. diss., Southwestern Baptist Theological Seminary, Fort Worth, Texas, 1931.

Mirandé, Alfredo. *The Chicano Experience: An Alternative Perspective.* South Bend: University of Notre Dame Press, 1985.

Montejano, David. *Anglos and Mexicans in the Making of Texas, 1836–1986.* Austin: University of Texas Press, 1987.

Murray, Andrew E. *The Skyline Synod: Presbyterianism in Colorado and Utah.* Denver: Golden Bell Press, 1971.

Náñez, Alfredo. "English-Speaking and Spanish-Speaking Methodism—One." Paper presented to the Special San Antonio Area Convocation on Missional Priorities, Travis Park UMC, San Antonio, October 5, 1978.

———. *Historia de la Conferencia Río Grande de la Iglesia Metodista Unida.* Dallas: Bridwell Library, Southern Methodist University, 1981.

————. "Methodism among the Spanish-Speaking People in Texas and New Mexico." In *One in the Lord: A History of Ethnic Minorities in the South Central Jurisdiction; The United Methodist Church,* by Walter Vernon, Alfredo Náñez, and John Graham, pp. 50–94. Oklahoma City: Commission on Archives and History, South Central Jurisdiction, The United Methodist Church, 1977.

Ortiz Vásquez, Dora. "Story of the Ocaté Bible." In *Sowers Went Forth,* by Ruth Barber and Edith Agnew, p. 21. Albuquerque: Menaul Historical Library of the Southwest, 1981.

Pitt, Leonard. *The Decline of the Californios: A Social History of the Spanish-Speaking Californians, 1846–1890.* Berkeley: University of California Press, 1970.

Pulido, Alberto López. *The Sacred World of the Penitentes.* Washington, DC: Smithsonian Institution Press, 2000.

Rendón, Gabino. "Mientras Miro los Años Pasar." Sermón memorial. Sermon preached at Bethel U.M. Church, September 20, 1961.

Sheridan, Thomas E. *Los Tucsonenses: The Mexican Community in Tucson, 1854–1941.* Tucson: University of Arizona Press, 1986.

Stapleton, Ernest S. "The History of Baptist Missions in New Mexico 1849–1866." Master's thesis, University of New Mexico, 1954.

Stratton, David. *The First Century of Baptists in New Mexico.* Albuquerque: The Woman's Missionary Union of New Mexico, 1954.

Survey of Service Organizations Represented in International Convention of Disciples of Christ. St. Louis: Christian Board of Publication, 1928.

Swartwout, Melba H. "Missionaries to Their Own People." *The Menaul Historical Review* 113, no. 3 (1986): 1–2.

Szasz, Ferenc Morton, *The Protestant Clergy in the Great Plains and Mountain West, 1865–1915.* Albuquerque: University of New Mexico Press, 1988.

Walker, Randi. *Protestantism in the Sangre de Cristos, 1850–1920.* Albuquerque: University of New Mexico Press, 1991.

Weber, David J. *Foreigners in Their Native Land: Historical Roots of the Mexican Americans.* Albuquerque: University of New Mexico Press, 1973.

————. *The Mexican Frontier, 1821–1846: The American Southwest Under Mexico.* Albuquerque: University of New Mexico Press, 1982.

Weatherby, Lela. "A Study of the Early Years of the Presbyterian Work with the Spanish Speaking People of New Mexico and Colorado and Its Development from 1850–1920." Master's thesis, Presbyterian College of Christian Education, Chicago, 1942.

Weigle, Marta. *Brothers of Lights, Brothers of Blood: The Penitentes of the Southwest.* Albuquerque: University of New Mexico Press, 1976.

Wicher, Eduard Arthur. *The Presbyterian Church in California, 1849–1927.* New York: Frederick H. Hitchcock; The Grafton Press, 1927.

Yohn, Susan M. *A Contest of Faiths: Missionary Women and Pluralism in the American Southwest.* Ithaca, N. Y.: Cornell University Press, 1995.

Zeleny, Carolyn. *Relations between the Spanish-Americans and Anglo-Americans in New Mexico.* New York: Arno Press, 1974.

Index